City Planning in America
BETWEEN PROMISE AND DESPAIR

Mary Hommann

PRAEGER

Westport, Connecticut
London

Library of Congress Cataloging-in-Publication Data

Hommann, Mary.
    City planning in America : between promise and despair / Mary
Hommann.
        p.   cm.
    Includes bibliographical references and index.
    ISBN 0-275-94473-5 (alk. paper)
    1. City planning—United States.   I. Title.
HT167.H66   1993
307.1'216'0973 – dc20   92-35351

British Library Cataloguing in Publication Data is available.

Library of Congress Catalog Card Number: 92-35351
ISBN: 0-275-94473-5

First published in 1993

Praeger Publishers, 88 Post Road West, Westport, CT 06881
An imprint of Greenwood Publishing Group, Inc.

Printed in the United States of America

The paper used in this book complies with the
Permanent Paper Standard issued by the National
Information Standards Organization (Z39.48-1984).

10 9 8 7 6 5 4 3 2 1

Dedicated to
Sustained Outrage

The Hottest Corners
of Hell are Reserved
for Those Who Keep Silent
in Times of
Moral Crisis.

(anonymous)

Contents

Acknowledgments

The author wishes to thank the following friends and former colleagues for their invaluable assistance in providing information or comments as this book was in preparation: Carol Carlton, John Mounts, David Popenoe, Natalie Safir, Marilyn Schurin, Marilyn Scott, Alan Turner, and Lucy Wynne Turner.

1

Opening Thesis

City planning is the art and science of civilization, at least in developmental terms. Its purpose is the physical and economic improvement of cities, towns, metropolitan regions, districts, and neighborhoods in a manner that will serve the greatest number. When planning is doing what it should, each new facility brings major benefits to a variety of users, even when their goals appear to conflict. City planning is properly undertaken by people who are objective, whose principal interest is the public good, who are trained to solve urban problems, and who are capable of thinking in terms of the whole when attempting to solve a part. By and large, a planner operates either as a consultant, supplying planning services to more than one jurisdiction, or as an employee of a municipality or county, part of the local government. This book for the most part addresses the fortunes of the latter—the local planner.

City planning in this country is quite new—primarily a profession of the twentieth century. This may be why considerable numbers of quite normal people have no concept of the nature and scope of city planning, if they have even a passing acquaintance with its very existence. As a twentieth-century profession, planning deals almost exclusively with built-up places, owned by myriad property owners, occupied by numerous lessees, experienced by countless neighbors and visitors. Developmental change, even when it favors the good of the community, is an extremely complex undertaking. This unwieldy assemblage is nevertheless the universe of the local planner.

Difficult though it may be to accomplish, urban planning is desperately needed in America. Well-executed planning is of great value to society. The fundamental problem is in America's body of laws which fails to empower the local planner. Even if the law sometimes requires that the local planner's advice be sought by other officials through "mandatory referral," it usually does not have to be followed. In controversial city planning matters the local planner never has the last word, unless someone in a position of power is in full agreement.

Although there have been occasional successes, by and large, American city planning is a profession that "solves problems" on paper, not in the real world. State constitutions and local charters give the power of decision-making to elected officials—mayors, boards of aldermen, and city councils—not to local planners. Thus, although urban development has galloped along freely throughout the century, little, if any, has been effected by city planners. In addition to elected officials, the people who have the power to affect the urban development universe are other politicians, real estate developers, and to some extent, state and federal officials.

In effect city planning is a profession created in the early 1900s to solve problems it was never permitted to solve. The post–World War II departure of businesses to surburban areas is a case in point. Despite the well-organized radial commuter rail systems that for decades in the first half century brought suburban workers into central cities, and despite vehement protests by concerned planners during the post-war period, bit by bit major cities have lost industry and commerce to residential suburbs. The results: for one thing, many suburban businesses are today unable to fill entry-level jobs (suburban teenagers can get higher-level jobs), while urban ghetto teenagers, desperate for work, have no way of getting to these outlying jobs unless the businesses happen to be close to railroad or bus stations or unless companies provide transportation. Another result of this suburban displacement is the incredible traffic congestion on the usually two-lane, two-way suburban road system, not designed for extensive crisscross circulation. In the absence of public transportation in these far-flung areas (which roads would be used for it anyway, and which of the scattered clients would it serve?), two-worker families drive two cars in congested and stalled traffic, and suburban economies suffer. All of this came about because of individual company choices and despite intelligent planning.

This lack of impact by planners on urban development is significant for our society. People trained to think through long-term problems in an impartial way and to develop functional solutions, beneficial to all groups, these people should be heard and respected in America, as they are in other democracies. With appropriate legal safeguards, many final decisions could be theirs. The operative concept here is *long-term*; rare is the elected administrator who has the will, or the luxury, to promote long-term solutions.

The problems and deficiencies of American city planning described throughout this book refer not only to the present day but also to what can

only be called the heyday of American planning, the period between 1949 and 1973. (President Richard Nixon terminated the urban renewal and other federal programs in early 1973.) As an index of that heyday: local planning jobs were plentiful indeed. Twice a month planners received a publication devoted solely to available jobs in planning—a periodical fat to bulging with employment opportunities nationwide. Compare that to today's handful of jobs, primarily upper-echelon, advertised in the monthly publication *Planning*. The early 1990s finds American city planning in a depression that has gradually worsened since 1973.

Heyday or not, that earlier planning period had major urban problems, and many are covered in this book. The reader may wonder whether these problems are relevant to the 1990s. They are. I pose the following as evidence: Think of a community-based project (not initiated by a developer) that you favored a few years ago when you first read about it in your local newspaper. OK, what happened to it?

Not only do virtually all the problems of those decades still exist, in most cases they have been exacerbated. Shopping centers and malls are still blithely destroying downtowns of established cities, public transit is still extremely inadequate, the choke of heavy motor traffic remains pronounced, overdevelopment continues to extrude in metropolitan centers; and still with us are those old favorites: land speculation, municipal corruption, and entrepreneurial greed.

As far back as 1962, the journalist Stewart Alsop agonized over the mess man-made America had become. Do these conditions sound familiar—three decades later?

Drive around the base of the cluster of concrete ant heaps, and you will see a littered, garish asphalt jungle. Look about you, at the bits of trash and garbage in the streets, the rust and peeling paint, the multicolored neon signs, endlessly winking on and off—GIANT BURGERS . . . KUSTOM KUT KLOTHES . . . EATS. Now drive slowly out from downtown. Within a few blocks, if your city is at all typical, you come on the "circle of decay," nearly universal in our cities.

The circle of decay consists of houses, once perhaps handsome and, alas, all too solidly built, which were occupied by merchants who used to walk to work in the days before the horseless carriage. Now they are musty funeral parlors, slatternly taverns, dubious boarding-houses. . . .

Beyond the circle of decay you are likely to find a newer area, a sort of no-man's land between the suburbs and the city proper. The no-man's land is a meaningless jumble—honky-tonks, gas stations with tinsel streamers, littered empty lots, glossy motels catering to the quick-turnover trade. Here you begin to see those terrible neon

arrows, plunging interminably downward toward some motel or eatery, blinding the eyes of the weary motorist. Here too begin the serried ranks of billboards, which stretch relentlessly on from your town to either coast, concealing and defiling the lovely land. . . .

Out of our closeness to the frontier there has grown, I think, an American cult of ugliness. When survival came first, a man who cared about beauty would be laughed or hounded out of town. Out of the frontier past has grown a subconscious consensus that there is something manly about messiness and ugliness, something sissified about whatever is handsome, or well ordered, or beautiful.

But the days of the frontier are gone, and more and more of us are going to have to live behind the same fixed borders. We are big boys now, and we must stop treating our country the way spoiled children treat their toys.[1]

One sentence seems to hark back to H. L. Mencken's amusing assertion that Americans are a race which "hates beauty as it hates truth . . . the love of ugliness for its own sake, the lust to make the world intolerable."[2]

Planning problems of the late twentieth century have indeed worsened the situation: widespread homelessness, the virtual absence of new low- and moderate-income housing, the burgeoning of amorphous "mega-suburbs" and "megacounties," and garbage gluttony. Of these, none is more horrific and shameful to our nation than homelessness—in gigantic proportions and growing daily.

Related socioeconomic problems of the late twentieth century include drastic reductions in social services for the poor, the ever-growing scarcity of unskilled and semi-skilled jobs, as electronic equipment continues to displace human labor (there is no going back here) and as the urban school fails to even minimally educate the ever-expanding urban under-class, urban and suburban crime, essentially caused by the need to support drug habits, in turn made more inevitable by unemployment.

According to the U.S. Department of Labor, in October 1990 black male unemployment, ages 25 to 34, was 3.0 times that of white males of the same age group. Black teenage unemployment, ages 16 to 19, was 2.3 times that of white teenagers and almost *6.0 times* higher than full-time unemployment for all groups.

Native Americans are worse off than blacks. Unbelievably, 35 percent were unemployed in 1987. They are less educated than any other ethnic group, and the jobs they do find pay low wages.[3]

Environmental problems have greatly increased of course in recent years: hazardous waste contamination, occupational and pesticide diseases, acid rain, deforestation, destruction of the ozone layer, the greenhouse effect, dangers from nuclear energy, gravely endangered

Garish Jumble of Highway Honky-Tonk, anytown U.S.A. (a)
(Photograph by Alan L. Scott)

Garish Jumble of Highway Honky-Tonk, anytown U.S.A. (b)
(Photograph by Alan L. Scott)

species, noise, air, water pollution, and more. The list is almost endless. The 1980s put much of America at risk.

The tragedy is that America's urban environment could have been one of ambiance and enjoyment. We have learned that from Europe. Perhaps it is worth examining here some of the developmental differences between American and European cities. Among the most arresting is the appearance of buildings, bridges, and other exterior man-made features, the general townscape experience. Parks and designed public spaces abound in European cities, and the banks of waterways are often enhanced for use by the public all along the route. Commonly, a lamppost is a work of art in Paris or Rome, as is a bridge or an arch, or sometimes the juxtaposition of a group of buildings. Color is used in every way, in the roof tiles, awnings, flowerboxes, and cafe tables. Of course, there are ugly industrial towns in Europe, but in general beauty exists in the cities and towns as much as in the countryside.

American cities have been built for commerce and utility more than as places in which citizens can live decently and enjoy themselves. Our waterways have for decades been virtually given over to industry, railroads, and expressways. In downtowns landowners have built buildings as tall and as broad (and as ugly) as they could get away with. American manufacturing and warehouse districts have become decayed, dreary, and unkempt. We are known to give a blind eye to slumlords who let properties deteriorate and default on basic services while still extracting high rents. The people who live in these hovels have fewer alternatives than ever.

Europe is beginning to copy the United States in its zeal for skyscrapers, but most buildings in European cities are quite low, the scale right for living. One of the most noticeable differences between European and American cities is the maintenance of townscape. The paving blocks of a street in the poorest section of Naples are as finely cut and attractive as those on the Via Veneto in Rome. Sidewalks are swept daily without exception. Vandalism of public townscape features is virtually unknown, and garbage cans are not crushed and broken by refuse collectors.

New York is not a truly civilized city, not in the sense that its people live close together in dignity and give attention and service to each other with cordiality, as they are accustomed to do in European metropolises. New York is an exploitative city. Almost from the beginning, its land, its harbors, its rivers, its very air, and a sizable portion of its people have been exploited. While every commercial enterprise may benefit the general public to some extent, in New York the balance between selfish interests and the public good has always been dramatically lopsided, to such an extent that many of its residents have become hopelessly hardened to it. And there is the pervasive ugliness of New York, the endless

Banks of Waterways Enhanced for Use by the Public All along the Route, Amsterdam
(Photograph by Natalie Safir)

Water's Edge Enjoyed by the Public, Paris
(Courtesy of the French Government Tourist Office)

Scale Right for Living, Amsterdam
(Photograph by Natalie Safir)

Scale Right for Living, Rome

masonry, the inharmonious development, the higgledy-piggledy utilitari-
anism, the virtual absence of prettiness except where there is wealth, and
the unrelenting "to hell with you" atmosphere that permeates everything.

New York streetscapes defy the term. Although in far worse condition
in the poorer districts, they are rarely attractive in any quarter.
Sophisticated New Yorkers, decked out in beautiful fashions, trip down
the sidewalks amidst blowing trash, over-patched paving, potholes, and
other discouraging features to reach the best restaurants and cabarets.
Doubtless they have convinced themselves that this handicap is but a
small price to pay for the total experience of living in America's most
exciting city.

In France and Italy the economy has been entrepreneurial for centuries, yet the needs of the city dwellers have obviously been kept in mind
in commercial endeavors. For every park and flowered area in these cities
there is a commercial establishment that enhances it, with graciousness
and taste. This is particularly true of cafes and restaurants introduced
into public areas and parks to serve human needs and sensibilities at
reasonable prices. Words like *simpatico* and *ambiance* are frequently
used to describe the pleasant and attractive man-made surroundings of
French and Italian cities.

"Planning is a reform movement," I used to declare, hoping we could
fuel it up. And in the mid-1950s everything seemed possible. The atmosphere was hopeful and electric. We idealists assumed we would just continue on a course of urban improvement until the whole job was com-
pleted nationwide. By 1963, however, I gave an editor the following
jaundiced view of the profession:

> I was interested in your editorial on planning and research in the
> November issue. Not only does the planning profession devote too
> much time to research—those who do engage in positive planning
> too often will not go through the ordeal of putting their ideas across.
> This kind of staff planner sees himself as advisor to the municipal
> administration, set apart from the grubbing of daily pushing and
> pulling.
>
> I suspect with sadness that there are many "planners" who don't
> care much about cities, who in their planning use only numbers and
> maps and rarely go out into the city and look at it. The city is
> dynamic and fluid; plans for it must be vital and full of life, and the
> planners must be too. But instead of a profession that is predomi-
> nantly vital, we seem to have a profession that is predominantly
> vapid.

"Advisor" means fighter. It means rallier of all the legitimately
conceivable forces to win—against politics, against ruthless business
tactics. It even means putting your job on the line sometimes for
something you believe in strongly. It means doing a lot of work plan-

Pleasant and Attractive Commercial Establishments: A Gas Station in Rome

The Needs of the City Dweller Kept in Mind in Commercial Establishments: A Cafe in Paris
(Courtesy of the French Government Tourist Office)

ners don't consider planning—getting into legal, financial, and administrative mechanics to promote planning ideas. It means understanding local politics, knowing how to maneuver the most important issues into acceptance, and compromising on the less important if you want anybody to listen to you.

And here we are at the main point of this letter. To get strong, tough action in towns that need a real revitalization job, a new type of position is being created right next to the mayor and right over planning, renewal, traffic, and all developmental departments. It usually goes by the name "development administrator" or some similar designation. These jobs, the biggest planning jobs in the country, are going to lawyers, political scientists, and public administrators. They go to people who know what to do to make renewal help the administration and the administration help renewal, but who may or may not learn about planning after they get the job. These jobs are not going to planners because planners won't learn the techniques and mechanics necessary to get things done, or concern themselves with the political needs of the municipal administration, and they are not going to planners also because no planners who have applied have what it takes to fill these vital positions.

Wouldn't it make more sense to have people ready to take these jobs who are fundamentally devoted to the cause of good city development and who learn administrative and political techniques in order to be effective? We are letting other professions fight for our goals, and if we don't get the right ones realized this way, we really have no grounds for complaint.[4]

To my knowledge no development administrator ever came out of the planning profession, despite this call to arms. Moreover, the third paragraph of this letter gives the sadly false impression that if an advisor turns fighter in the manner described, he or she will be rewarded with a "win." Such implementation of plans is only possible in the rarified atmosphere of a well-funded and unusually enlightened local administration ready and able to take some major risks (for example, New Haven, Connecticut, under Mayor Richard C. Lee and the federal renewal programs of the 1950s and 1960s). Even these heroic efforts have been sporadic and temporary.

How are American planners doing today? When there is an opening for a local planner in even a small city, the number of applicants for the job can be in the hundreds. Graduate planning schools, for reasons that are unclear, are staying open, sometimes teaching real estate! Some seem to pride themselves on getting jobs for their graduates in the private sector—in investment banking firms, rating firms, real estate development companies, brokerage houses, insurance companies, and banks.[5] In my opinion, this practice is a degenerate distortion of the basic goal of city planning. Moreover, from the practical standpoint, the private sector provides no career path for a true urban planner. He or she faces daily frustration within such a structure. The only choice here is to metamorphose or get out. In local government the only planner who is in any way effective is the chief, the planning director. Thus even within a local planning agency a young graduate planner can accomplish very little. But within this context he is at least on a realistic career path. A motivated junior planner in the private sector has about the effectiveness potential of a hen in the fox house.

Psychologists have given us the concept of denial—a state of mind in which a person convinces himself that what is happening is not happening. The satisfied planner of today is experiencing an advanced case of denial.

This book is an attempt to demonstrate the following: that, although desperately needed, generally speaking urban planning has no effect on urban development in this country, where developers are supreme; that this is because urban planning has not been legally organized to make a difference; that at best local planners are exposed daily to the fiction of their involvement in developmental decisions; that many city planners, finding themselves professionally impotent, engage in alternate or deviant pursuits. The book also sets out to show that greed settled this country, accompanied by cruelty, disregard, and callous misjudgment; that these qualities have continued to control economic and settlement decisions, accompanied in this century by criminal conspiracy; that millions of our people live in desperate conditions economically, many without decent shelter, or any shelter, pointing to the need for government to directly supply housing, as has been done for decades in Western European countries; and that urban planning has been capable, in control, and ongoing in European democracies for almost half a century, demonstrating the kind of difference planning could make in America if similar legal policies were adopted.

In the interest of comprehension, a few words are in order about the various actors in this collection of urban fields loosely lumped together under the planning banner. American generalist planners need not be trained as architects or engineers, as they must in some Western countries. Masters degrees in planning usually require two years of full-time study. Development planners are generalists who focus primarily on key developments, often in downtowns, which are intended to spearhead the turnaround of a declining city.

Designers, that is architects, landscape architects, and urban designers, have been designing cities for centuries, and on the Continent today few, if any, planners are not also architects. In this country architects think nothing of identifying themselves as "architects and planners." This can be a problem when they are neither trained as planners nor committed to the economic and social research that is a necessary part of modern city planning. Designers have been known to avoid vital market studies, with dire results. On the positive side, designers who practice planning are normally deeply concerned about what happens within their scope of interest and can be counted on to push for *results*.

There are urban experts who drift into the field when funding is plentiful, often becoming known as planners, sometimes ending up as developers. These people usually start out as lawyers, political scientists, public administrators, housing experts, or untrained political appointees.

Engineers usurped American planning for many years. Disdained by generalist planners for their narrow urban vision, engineers in planning tend to limit themselves to practical spatial layouts and nuts-and-bolts issues.

The product of the social planner consists of services, such as day-care programs, job-training programs, and the like. Developing-nations planners manifestly focus on the very specialized scope of planning for developing nations. Advocacy planning is a single-issue approach to planning in which the planner becomes a fighter for a cause. (To me, "single issue" and "city planning" are mutually exclusive concepts.) Economists specializing in cities call themselves economic planners.

Traffic and transportation planners are usually traffic engineers. Traffic planners created tremendous problems in twentieth-century urban development, and generalist planners permitted this crisis to develop by disassociating themselves from this vital element of urban growth and change. Chapter 9 is devoted to this issue.

The only urban professional trained to look at the whole picture and to strive for balance is the generalist planner. Tragically, in America's planning climate a substantial number of generalists have become obstructionists, as may be seen in Chapter 6.

For this planner: my forty-year professional life has been spent primarily as a generalist and development planner, working in a variety of areas, including local planning, urban renewal, county planning, planning education, federal planning, and consultant planning. My graduate education was achieved through the University of Pennsylvania School of Fine Arts in the 1950s, when Dean G. Holmes Perkins brought to that school faculty members that were considered among the supreme planning thinkers of the nation. Although I hold high standards of professional integrity, thoroughness, and scholarship, I have also been accurately described both as a "to-the-ramparts planner" and one who is "capable of sustained outrage." This book will certainly attest to the latter.

In reading this book, it should be remembered that (1) it is not about huge metropolitan cities like New York, unless so noted, but primarily about small and middle-sized cities of from 30,000 in population to, say, 800,000; (2) it refers to cities that really need help, and (3) tremendous citizen support for planning is often found in cities that need very little help, relatively speaking. Conversely, the more a city needs planning, the less support it seems to get from the community.

Planning used to be called "city planning." Then in the 1960s it was changed in some quarters to "urban planning." It is still common, however, for a city's planning agency to be called the "city planning department." Very confusing. The reader may read "city planning" as "urban planning" and vice versa, in most cases.

The term "local planner" as used herein should be understood as "planning director," even though other planners may well be on the planning staff.

For the sake of simplicity, the term "mayor" is frequently used herein for local chief administrator, and the term "city council" used for most local governing bodies, even though positions and titles vary according to state and local charters and laws.

Because American planning deals primarily with built-up places and existing institutions, to the planner these represent the universe to be addressed. Often they constitute problems to overcome, patterns to be changed, conditions to be improved. Therefore, how American cities became the way they are today is the subject of Chapter 2.

NOTES

1. Stewart Alsop, "America the Ugly, Our Once-Lovely Land Has Become a Garish, Tasteless, Messy Junk Heap," *Saturday Evening Post* (June 23, 1962), pp. 9-10.

2. H. L. Mencken, *Prejudices, Sixth Series* (New York: Alfred A. Knopf, 1927), p. 193.

3. "Native Americans Adrift in Their Own Land," *Time* (July 6 ,1987), p. 89.

4. Mary S. Hommann, "Letter to the Editor," *Pratt Planning Papers* (April 1963), p. 2.

5. Elizabeth M. Fowler, "Careers: Emergence of City Planning," *New York Times* (April 10, 1985).

2

Historic Survey of American Development

What the City Planner Has to Deal With

This chapter is not about planning. It sets the stage for a discussion of planning in America. It is about the people who settled and governed this young democracy, how they treated the vast, immensely resourceful continent they had acquired, and how they treated Native Americans, Africans, East European workers, and others in their efforts to build America and in some cases enrich themselves. It addresses our economic and social legacies, and it brings attention to the successes and failures of self-government, settlement patterns, and housing development. Much of what was built in the past remains today. The dysfunctional portions of this universe are what city planning wanted to do something about when it came into being in the latter part of the nineteenth century and still must deal with today. How the planning profession has been able to meet the challenge is the subject of Chapter 3.

First encountered as a magnificent virgin wilderness, much of America has been transformed into a chaotic agglomeration of masonry, steel, signboards, and slurb. Only a fraction of man-made development has been beautifully designed and maintained, and this has been created primarily for the affluent.

Early North Atlantic coast townships, settled primarily by British colonists, were simple, clean, and efficient. Buildings were grouped attractively around a village green, the dual purpose of which was community marketplace and cattle pasture. Typically, farmland radiated out from the center on long, narrow lots. A few central lots were set aside for meeting house, school, and burial ground.

New England towns are likened to medieval villages in their organic unity and instinctive planning. Although early architecture had strong medieval characteristics, attached houses were not the norm; township houses stood quite far apart. In Virginia the courthouse town consisted of a handsome courthouse, a tiny open space, several churches, and perhaps a library or lawyer's office.

Early New England policies required that all house lots be occupied before families could settle away from townships. As a town became the desired size, town fathers restricted growth and spawned a new township some miles distant. This example of what today would be town planning gold is tarnished when we realize that the policy was enforced in some towns by fining the visitor who refused to leave or by flogging the naked body if that visitor were without funds.

By 1680 the agricultural market town became the prevalent form in all the colonies, with farmers living on their land away from centers. Houses were scattered throughout the countryside, a pattern even more pronounced in the South. Town centers became the domain of artisans, lawyers, and merchants, and the daily life of a large New England town took place as much in the harbor as in the marketplace.

Both church and colonial authorities preferred tight communities but were no match for the spirit of individualism and the craving for land. With tremendous toil, early Americans fought against the wilderness, hacking virtually every settlement and farm out of the forest. Perhaps because of the folly of widespread tree elimination, every colonial town was ultimately embellished with elegant rows of street trees. Foreign visitors spoke admiringly of the neat symmetry of urban tree-lined streets. The white church steeple that today symbolizes the New England village actually was not introduced until 1740.

Probably as a result of London's new gridded street plan for a section of the city following the great fire of 1666, virtually every community in America was laid out on a gridiron street plan after 1670, with almost every street, by definition, either parallel or at right angles to every other. Boston's winding streets can be attributed to its settlement in 1630. There were occasional attempts at grandeur in early American planning, but Williamsburg and Savannah may be the only examples of American Baroque. Pierre Charles L'Enfant's elegant plan for Washington was an ultimately successful attempt to break away from the grid, but most such attempts were not realized. Philadelphia was planned in 1682 by William Penn with gridded streets and five public squares. Savannah, too, was developed with several urban parks and squares. Virtually all other towns relinquished public squares, or failed to plan for them, as the pressures of development and speculation persisted.

Foreign visitors found colonial Americans to be a hardworking, sober lot—religionists for the most part. Except for a few free spirits like Benjamin Franklin, colonial Americans were probably boring people by twentieth-century standards. One impression stands out: However kindly they might have been in individual cases, European settlers assumed in their heart of hearts that they were superior to the red man and to the black man, and that their settlement needs and economic desires had to predominate in any contest with these peoples. Because the Christian religion was "infinitely superior" to pagan beliefs, because their culture and technology were significantly more advanced, it only followed, they assumed, that European-Americans were more advanced themselves.

European settlers treated America as vacant land. Some Indians were friendly and helpful to settlers, and some stoutly defended their territory. It made no difference. Indians were uprooted and pushed west unceasingly. King George III's Proclamation of 1763, for example, reserved land west of the Appalachian Mountains for the Indians and prohibited general colonial settlement there. Less than five years later the Proclamation line was officially moved west, as various treaties were negotiated with the tribes, the first of hundreds that were made and broken over the years by European-Americans. Frontiersmen made liberal use of rum and whiskey to befuddle Indians into agreements. When in 1831 the Cherokee Nation tried to enlist the aid of the U.S. Supreme Court to compel the State of Georgia to recognize *federal* treaties, the court refused to act, on the self-serving and spurious grounds that the Cherokee were not a "foreign nation" but a "dependent nation." In other words, Indians had no freedom of choice and no control over their own destinies. It could be said that European-Americans had nothing against the American natives; they just wanted to settle on their lands with a minimum of interference and expense.

> We did not think of the great open plains, the beautiful rolling hills, and winding streams with tangled growth, as "wild." Only to the white man was nature a "wilderness" and only to him was the land "infested" with "wild" animals and "savage" people. To us it was tame. Earth was bountiful and we were surrounded with the blessings of the Great Mystery.[1]

> The White people never cared for land or deer or bear. When we Indians kill meat, we eat it all up. When we dig roots we make little holes. When we built houses, we make little holes. When we burn grass for grasshoppers, we don't ruin things. We shake down acorns and pinenuts. We don't chop down the trees. We only use dead wood. But the White people plow up the ground, pull down the trees, kill everything. The tree says, "Don't. I am sore. Don't hurt me." But they chop it down and cut it up. The spirit of the land hates them. They blast out trees and stir it up to its depths. They saw up the trees. That hurts them. The Indians never hurt anything, but the White people destroy all.[2]

Although the first twenty Africans arrived at Jamestown in 1619 as indentured servants, slavery was legally recognized after 1650. One wonders
what would have happened if significant attention had been paid to some
concrete suggestions made at the time to pay indentured servants, usually
European, to undertake the extensive and pressing agricultural work of
the South. Some thought it would cost about the same, since indentured
servants would be responsible for their own living expenses. The concept
did not prevail, and by 1690 African slaves became the major source of
cheap labor in the southern colonies, completely replacing indentured
servants. Several million Africans were enslaved and brought to America
in chains over the three centuries. Many died en route as a result of
unspeakable shipboard conditions.

During the American Revolution, the vast majority of Americans con-
ducted life as usual and ignored the war. "Sunshine patriots" even sold
food to the enemy while General Washington's relatively small band of
tattered soldiers were near starvation. Under these circumstances, it is as-
tonishing that independence was ever won. "The spirit of venality is the
most dreadful and alarming enemy America has to oppose," said John
Adams during this period. "This predominant avarice will ruin America, if
she is ever ruined. . . . I am ashamed of the age I live in."[3]

A census was taken in 1790, one year after the inauguration of George
Washington as the nation's first president. It revealed a population of
about 4 million, of which approximately 50 percent were in the South, 25
percent in the Middle Colonies, and 25 percent in the North. The census
figure included about 800,000 slaves. Indians were not even counted. The
urban population numbered little more than 215,000, with Philadelphia's
count of 42,000 the largest.

The colonial period can be said to have influenced today's development
in three significant ways: First, slavery of Africans was established on a
massive scale. This created a doctrine of racism and a pattern of great
wealth based on the exploitation of other human beings. In developmental terms, these patterns resulted in the establishment of spectacular
mansions for the rich and squalid housing for the poor and black,
ultimately leading to urban ghettos. Second, the devastation of Native
Americans and the confiscation of their territories were instituted. Europeans settled towns wherever they thought best, giving little consideration to Indian territorial rights. If peaceful Indian settlements got in the
way, no retreat was collectively contemplated; the matter was one of
determining the easiest and surest method of extrication. Third, the
mechanical and commercial gridiron street system for towns and cities
was introduced. An urban street system, once developed, can of course be
changed only with tremendous difficulty, and the gridiron is therefore
with us today in great profusion.

Speculation was rampant even during the American Revolution. There
was speculation and profiteering in Army contracts, and securities sold to

patriots to finance the war were bought up by speculators for a fraction of their face value. In 1778 George Washington despaired of the "speculation, peculation, and insatiable thirst for riches" that seemed to "have got the better of every other consideration and almost every order of men."[4]

After the war was won, a primary concern of the Continental Congress became the settlement of its war debt. In the reckless rush to sell public lands, the vast region northwest of the Ohio River was to be disposed of at as good a price and as quickly as possible. Under the provisions of the Land Ordinance of 1785, a beautiful land of forests and streams, gentle valleys and hills was to be apportioned by T-square and triangle, carved into an enormous gridiron. The ordinance provided that all land be divided into townships exactly six miles square, townships almost twice the size of New York's Manhattan. Each township was to be divided into thirty-six lots ("sections") of one square mile each, and a family was required to buy a minimum of one lot—that is, a rectangular plot as large as 75 percent of New York's Central Park.[5] One lot of each township was to be for a common school, and four other lots were to be reserved for the national government. The ordinance required that streets follow the rectangular lot lines, regardless of geology or contour. Land speculation was prohibited, but because the minimum price was $641 a lot and the land auctions took place only in the East, individual sales were relatively few. These unrealistic requirements manifestly encouraged speculation, first by the Ohio Company of Associates, which bought 1.5 million acres for its own members at $1 an acre on long payment terms, and second by the notorious Scioto Company, which bought 3.5 million acres, splitting the lots into sizes people could readily afford but maintaining the rectangular shapes.

Surprisingly, the Land Ordinance of 1785 was conceived by Thomas Jefferson, America's first Renaissance man, someone who encouraged the rural life, who spoke repeatedly of the "health, virtue, and freedom" of the farm. No interest seems to have been taken at the time in the artificial and mechanical effect that this monster gridiron development would have on the country. But the speculators knew.

> Still another cornerstone of national planning for the West, the Land Ordinance of 1785, derived from Jefferson's conception and revealed, once again, his passion for rational order and precision. The effects of the rectilinear land survey projected by this legislation are visible even today to anyone who flies over the prairies and plains and observes the linear patchwork of the fields below.[6]

John W. Reps comments as well on American's vast checkerboard:

> With military precision, modified only on occasion by some severe topographic break, or some earlier system of land distribution, this

rectangular grid persists to the shores of the Pacific. America thus lives on a giant gridiron imposed on the natural landscape by the early surveyors carrying out the mandate of the Continental Congress expressed in the Land Ordinance of 1785. . . . Perhaps the rectangular survey pattern for the west was the only system that could have resulted in speedy settlement and the capture of a continent for the new nation, but its results in city planning were dullness and mediocrity.[7]

What is particularly unfathomable is the perpetuation over the next century of Jefferson's "passion for rational order and precision." For although subsequent land laws were liberalized with respect to minimum size of parcel purchased, price, and the methods of acquisition and resale, the lots still had to be rectangular. Furthermore, the congressional objective of land disposal, something to be got rid of as easily as possible, seems to have prevailed right up through the Homestead Act of 1862. Between 1870 and 1880 this act brought an area the size of Great Britian into cultivation. Not surprisingly, although designed by Congress to provide land for small farms, fraudulent lumber and mining companies bought up vast areas for commercial profit. Under the Homestead Act, land price was put at $1.25 an acre after six months of individual family residence and cultivation, and it was free after five years.

Returning to the 1780s, political settlement of the area west of the Ohio River was to be governed by the Northwest Ordinance of 1787, one of the marvels of the Continental Congress. Based on a plan of Thomas Jefferson's, this complex settlement law assured religious freedom, public education, and the prohibition of slavery in that western area.

The winter of 1786-87 saw America in chaos. "Social revolt was a reality in the East, and in the Southwest secession was openly threatened. States were jealous of one another and childishly quarrelsome; rivalry went beyond all bounds of common sense, and the masses hated the classes."[8] George Washington warned as early as 1783: "It is yet to be decided whether the Revolution must ultimately be considered as a blessing or a curse."[9] Britain's Dean of Gloucester found idle and visionary any notion that Americans could form together a powerful nation under one head:

The mutual antipathies and clashing interests of the Americans, their difference of governments, habitudes, and manners, indicate that they will have no center of union and no common interest. They never can be united into one compact empire under any species of government whatever; a disunited people till the end of time, suspicious and distrustful of each other, they will be divided and subdivided into little commonwealths or principalities, according to natural boundaries, by great bays of the sea, and by vast rivers, lakes and ridges of mountains.[10]

Through the tremendous efforts of a handful of people, notably Alexander Hamilton and James Madison, the Constitutional Convention was convened in May of 1787. George Washington was unanimously elected president in 1789.

Had our first president appointed James Madison his first secretary of the treasury instead of Alexander Hamilton (which may never have been contemplated), the United States might well have developed into a very different country, a nation of small and middle-sized capitalists, artisans, professionals, and workers, rather than one of extremes of great wealth and poverty—at least for a time. Through the funding-assumption bill Hamilton created the fundamental mechanisms and climate for the oligarchical capitalism that triumphed during the Industrial Revolution and that we still have today. In addition, he encouraged and enhanced speculation. Speculation in land has been responsible in part for the creation of ugly towns and cities throughout the country, and it has distorted our land use policies over and over again. Hamilton was assisted in the passage of the funding-assumption bill by Thomas Jefferson and James Madison through the acceptance of a quid pro quo, possibly the first major act of political horse trading to occur in the young nation. It happened in the summer of 1790.

Several months earlier Congress asked the young and brilliant treasury secretary to address the new nation's financial question. To Hamilton the establishment of the United States Government as a central power, supreme over the states, was of primary importance. This required first, the establishment of the nation's credit and second, the creation of a United States Bank. None of this could be considered before the $75 million war debt was paid. Resulting from the powerlessness of the Continental Congress to levy taxes, the war debt consisted of $42 million owed to patriots who had bought securities to finance the war (we would call them bonds), $12 million owed to France, Holland, and Spain, and about $21 million owed in states' debts. To complicate things, some of the states remained in debt, while others, the southern states except South Carolina, had already arranged for payment. Submitted to Congress in February of 1790, the assumption portion of Hamilton's funding-assumption bill provided for the payment by the federal government only of those state debts remaining unpaid. The funding portion called for the payment of face value of the securities to those holding them, largely speculators who had bought them for a fraction of face value, rather than the original citizen buyers.

According to Miller, Hamilton privately admired speculators and thought he needed them for the kind of national economy he envisioned.

To him, capitalism did not involve modest entrepreneurial undertakings organized and directed by individual owner-managers. Capitalism meant great wealth in the hands of the audacious few.

Although he did not say so on his Report on Public Credit, Hamilton's attitude toward the men who were engaged in engrossing the national debt had undergone a sea change since the days of the Revolutionary War. The righteous warmth of that earlier period had been succeeded by a coldly realistic view of the advantages of speculation and concentration of wealth in a capitalistic economy. In many respects, the speculators were men after his own heart: these were the kind of capitalists he wished to see take over the direction of the national economy. At a time when the government's credit had almost reached the vanishing point, they had staked their money upon a hazard the success of which "turned on little less than a revolution in government." Men willing to risk their wealth on long chances he deemed indispensable to a flourishing capitalism; he liked his capitalism spiced with audacity and he found this particular ingredient abundantly among the purchasers of government securities. Moreover, with a perspicacity not always evidenced by twentieth-century statesmen, Hamilton saw that if capitalism were to prosper, capitalists were indispensable. Since he knew of no effective substitute for capitalism, he believed that one of the principal duties of government dedicated to the general welfare was to foster capitalism by affording every facility to the accumulation of wealth. And, since the United States had few large aggregations of capital, Hamilton thought that the government ought to take an active part in creating wealth and in making sure that it got into the hands of those able to make the best use of it.

Thus, from Hamilton's point of view, an equal distribution of the government's largesse would not have advanced his purpose. As David Hume had observed, capital was of comparatively little value to the economy and to the state "if it is dispersed into numberless hands, which either squander it in idle show and magnificence, or emply it in the purchase of the common necessaries of life." Hamilton was primarily concerned with those individuals who possessed a disposable surplus of capital which could be devoted to the support of the government and to the furthering of economic enterprise. To an eighteenth-century statesman bent upon creating the conditions in which capitalism could flourish, the "improvident majority" was of little importance.[11]

James Madison, the young congressman from Virginia (ultimately the nation's fourth president), actively opposed the funding-assumption bill on moral grounds. He wanted the original patriot purchasers—widows, orphans, and former soldiers—to be paid for the securities, rather than the exploitative speculators, and he wanted *all* state war debts, both paid and unpaid, to be assumed by the federal government.

> Madison had no confidence in a government that depended upon avarice for its principal support. . . . [He] feared that if advantage were given to "the sagacious, the enterprising, and the moneyed few over the industrious and uninformed mass of the people," the few would oppress the many. He recoiled from the "impatient avidity for immediate and immoderate gain" in which Hamilton saw a potent force that might be made to work in the interests of union.[12]

But the House of Representatives found justice too expensive—all that bookkeeping and searching of old records to find original security-purchasers, to say nothing of the overwhelming cost of assuming the war debts of states already debt-free or close to it. Much as Congress admired the humanitarian and virtuous Gentleman from Virginia (strong representatives were "seen to weep" during his funding-bill speeches on the House floor) that body defeated Madison's plan by a wide margin. It is always cheaper to cut corners.

Speculation in 1789 and 1790 knew no bounds. However, some of those who bought up securities by the bundle in the autumn of 1789 may well have been acting on a sure thing, tipped off as to Hamilton's projected report by his shady assistant secretary of the treasury, William B. Duer. A significant figure in the Scioto land speculation of 1787, Duer resigned as early as April 1790, apparently to save his own skin. That Hamilton knew of Duer's suspect dealings before he appointed him is certain, according to Miller, although Hamilton took great care to conduct his own financial life with perfect rectitude. While Congress was considering Hamilton's report early in 1790, speculators went to the length of chartering ships to reach the southern states before news of the secretary's report could reach southern cities. And during the subsequent six or seven months in which the bill languished, the speculators went wild.

> Much of the frenzied buying and selling the spring of 1790 was the work of a relatively small number of speculators. Because of the strong opposition encountered in Congress by Hamilton's report, wary security holders began to hedge against a possible failure of the funding-assumption bill. As a consequence of this hedging, the impression was created that a large amount of new securities, fresh from the hands of the original holders, was being thrown upon the market. But it was closer to the truth to say, as was remarked at the

time, that the speculators "vulture-like, are looking out to see where they shall *perch* to the greatest advantage." As they fluttered about from state to federal securities and back again, following the trend of the voting in Congress, the air seemed filled with speculators— with the result, said Hamilton, that "a few hundred thousand dollars appeared like as many millions."[13]

As a result of his insistence that the funding and assumption proposals remain joined, Hamilton was actually risking the very solvency of the new nation and its creditors. That he truly believed in his plan is not in question. He found hope in the realization that each time the bill was rejected by the House, it lost by a small margin. All he needed was a little leverage.

On the point of desperation in June of that year, Hamilton attempted to persuade the prominent Virginian, Thomas Jefferson, secretary of state, to throw his weight behind the bill. There is little doubt that Hamilton had in mind the potential promise of using his own influence in locating a new U.S. capital on the Potomac River—a prospect the Virginians longed for—in return for their help in passing the funding-assumption bill. (The capital was situated temporarily in New York at the time). In speaking eloquently to Jefferson that night in front of the president's house, however, the only subject reportedly broached was the saving of the Union. The denouement of this little drama is that it was probably the Virginians, Jefferson and Madison, who first broached the subject of a trade-off and set the price for their influence in getting Hamilton's bill passed: the nation's capital permanently situated on the Potomac in ten years. The bill passed.[14]

Although Jefferson later claimed prior ignorance of the contents of the funding-assumption bill, Miller finds this claim untenable, as do Mitchell and Peterson.[15] There is no doubt, however, that he regretted most grievously his part in the nation's first congressional log-rolling in which the plutocrats triumphed and the people went empty-handed.

Jefferson soon came to regret his part in this sectional bargain as the worst error of his political life. He had been "duped" by the Secretary of Treasury and "ignorantly and innocently made to hold the candle" for his fraudulent scheme to throw $20,000,000 or more of state debts to "the stock-jobbing herd." His national feelings had been enlisted to forward a system far more injurious to the Union, he came to believe, than the selfishness of congressmen and speculators whose threats Hamilton had so cleverly used to fan his fears in 1790.[16]

Thus in the interest of building a rich and powerful nation, Hamilton worked from the start to place wealth in the hands of the speculators—to foster risk-taking capitalists who would both support the national government and pursue industrial enterprise. With the passage of the funding-assumption bill the egalitarian economy of modest enterprise and agriculture was plowed under, and this was done with the assistance of the very statesmen who advocated an egalitarian economy and despised speculation, oppression by the moneyed few, and other fundamentals of oligarchical capitalism.

Inexorably, these economic forces began to reshape the cities, as pleasant urban life gave way to utility and commerce. New York was a dramatic case in point. Following independence the city's lovely and numerous street trees were chopped down for firewood during a cold snap—vandalized one by one—until virtually all were gone. Rudofsky finds it ironic that the constellation of urban dignity, beauty, and charm that twentieth-century Americans eagerly cross the Atlantic to see on summer vacations once was ours. But in the short space of two generations a "total wreck," an "oblivion of the entire city," appears to have taken place.[17]

Perhaps the greatest insult to New York in the name of "city planning" was the Commissioners' Plan of 1811, which gridded the entire city from Chambers Street to 155th Street in long rectangular blocks and numerous crosstown streets. Following this street layout, hills were leveled and ponds, springs, and brooks filled in. Gone were irregular lots, flower gardens, small orchards, shady lanes, beautiful boulders, and escarpments. A "Jubilation of Destruction" took place, as Manhattan was transformed over the succeeding years into a "wasteland of streets."[18] Only Broadway broke the pattern as development occurred. Because the perfectly rectangular parcels of land could be bought, sold, and registered promptly, Manhattan became a magnet to avaricious Americans from every part of the Union eager to make fortunes on land speculation and overdevelopment. Except in rare instances, the market value of New York's land quickly became too high to allow civic beauty or pleasant city life to become part of the equation. The Commissioners' "Plan" of 1811 marked the beginning of Manhattan's continuous and relatively rapid cycle of destruction and redevelopment for greater density and astronomical profits. Through creative planning, the greenness and charm of the Colonial city could have been preserved to coexist with prosperity, progress, and modern construction. But this was not to be.

Passionate objections came from all quarters, to no avail. The plan called for very few parks because of the "large arms of the sea which embrace Manhattan Island"—an ironic point, as commercial and industrial wharves, and later highways, were allowed to take over almost every foot of waterfront.[19] Ah, but what about Central Park? Obliteration and development had not reached as far north as 59th Street in 1854 when the idea of a sizable park became a mayoral campaign issue. Only a few squatter huts had to be pulled down to make way for Olmstead and Vaux's great masterpiece. Today, with Manhattan development having extended beyond the wildest nightmares of the 1850s, this beautiful park of 843 acres has become, to many New Yorkers, Manhattan's saving grace.

Edgar Allan Poe mourned with considerable anguish the effects of the commercial gridiron on New York in a letter written to the newspaper *Columbia Spy* in 1844:

> Some of the most picturesque sites for villas to be found within the limits of Christendom . . . are doomed. The spirit of Improvement has withered them with its acrid breath. Streets are already "mapped" through them, and they are no longer suburban residences, but "town lots." In some thirty years every noble cliff will be a pier, and the whole island will be densely desecrated by buildings of brick, with portentous *facades* of brownstone . . . I could not think of the magnificent cliffs, and stately trees, which at every moment met my view, without a sign for their inevitable doom—inevitable and swift. In twenty years, or thirty at farthest, we shall see here nothing more romantic than shipping, warehouses and wharves."[20]

The gridiron street pattern and land speculation relentlessly go hand in hand. Speculation in land turns human environment, the earth itself, into one vast salable commodity, to be played with like cards or roulette wheels. Speculation unremittingly encourages the spiraling of land costs, the destruction of sound buildings, and their replacement with everbigger, higher income-producing constructions.

On the subject of the gridiron plan and speculation, the views of Tunnard and Reed are clear:

> The overwhelming presence of business is emphasized in the plans of American cities. The skyscraper is one symbol, the gridiron plan another. There are parallel and right-angled streets in every community. With a few exceptions which serve to confirm the rule, the cities of America have been laid out mercilessly "by the compass," as James Fenimore Cooper observed, and no hill, no lake, no river or other natural obstacle bends the straight line. . . . In some countries, such as France and Italy, the aim is to own and to hold; in the United States it is to own and to speculate.[21]

Lewis Mumford was a strong advocate of organic planning, in which the city plan evolves gradually in response to human needs—as it did in medieval cities. He is outraged by the commercial gridiron system of town design. He terms it the "speculative ground plan":

This plan offers an engineer none of those special problems that irregular parcels and curved boundary lines present. An office boy could figure out the number of square feet involved in a street opening or in a sale of land: even a lawyer's clerk could write a description of the necessary deed of sale, merely by filling in with the proper dimensions the standard document. . . .

Such plans fitted nothing but a quick parcelling of the land, a quick conversion of farmsteads into real estate, and a quick sale. The very absence of more specific adaptations to landscape or to human purpose only increased, by its very indefiniteness and designlessness its general usefulness for exchange. Urban land, too, now became a mere commodity, like labor: its market value expressed its only value.[22]

These gridiron plans have a frequently-touted pedestrian advantage: ready comprehension by a city's newcomers who can avoid getting lost. And they may have one positive townscape characteristic when applied to steep hill towns—spectacular natural views at the ends of streets. But such benefits cannot fairly be said to balance out the evils. Artistically, these plans are consummately uninspired. Too often they have been applied to hilly American towns—streets cut right across the crests of precipitous hills, resulting in houses perched up in the air on one side of a street, with thirty-step "front walks," and the roofs of houses "across the street" barely visible down the hill. And although San Francisco gets wide praise as a handsome city, the source of this view is surely not its gridiron street plan. Mumford speaks of the costs in wasted energy and time to San Franciscans, of economic losses measurable in wasted fuel, not to mention the loss in beautiful townscape experiences that would have been known to them had the city been platted intelligently, respecting the contours of the land. He implies that San Francisco would have been organically planned had city fathers not rejected the advice of Frederick Law Olmstead in 1865. Organic planning of steep sites calls for curving, irregular streets like those of Assisi, Siena, and San Gimignano in Italy. In Siena, as Mumford observes, a winding street will be intersected at intervals to provide an opening for a stunning view or a steep flight of stairs.[23]

An irregular street pattern can be a delightful townscape experience on even terrain, as well. In Paris, for instance, a typical street turns to left or right every 200 to 300 feet, providing pedestrians with one or two buildings to observe as they walk. Perfect sites for architecture are everywhere.

Mumford maintains that from the sixteenth century onward in Europe, the organic city had to give way to the commercial city, the capitalist city. Divorcing itself from a sense of social responsibility or the serving of human needs, the capitalist city served to authorize slum housing:

Instead of being penalized for his antisocial exploitation of land, the slum landlord, on capitalist principles, was handsomely rewarded:

for the values of his decayed properties, so far from being written off because of their age and disrepair, became embedded in the structure of land values and taxes. . . .

The more dense the occupation, the higher the income: the higher the income, the higher the capitalizable value of the land.[24]

Mumford finds that capitalism has turned every corner of the city into a negotiable commodity. Capitalism brought a new kind of urban order, in which business "took precedence over every other kind of activity." No section of the city was planned for its specific function. "The only function considered was the progressive intensification of use, for the purpose of meeting expanding business needs and raising land values."[25]

This approach to urban land brought unheard of congestion, particularly in the quarters of the poor. When capitalism became dominant and exclusive, "commercial success" in urban development "showed itself for what it was, and still largely is: civic destitution."[26]

In terms of the economic and land development of America, the nineteenth century was extraordinary. The century of brave pioneering, miraculous invention, steam power, soaring enterprise, the Industrial Revolution, abolition of slavery, and wave upon wave of immigration was also the century of exaggerated land speculation, smoky urban filth, unbridled railroad extortion, miserable housing, oppression of ethnic groups, engulfing greed, beyond-belief municipal corruption, and hell-on-earth working conditions.

Very few, if any, American Indians benefited from the European invasion of their continent. Smelser testifies to their fate in the early decades of the century:

East of the Mississippi the country was booming. Only the Indians (and a few arch-Federalists) regretted it. About seventy thousand Indians lived there. They had known three sets of masters, French, British, and American, in forty years. Six-sevenths of them lived in the Old Southwest. They were debauched by private traders, peonized by government factories, policed by soldiers, and governed by incompetent agents and distracted, empty-handed territorial governors. Most palefaces thought they should go West or drop dead, but Jefferson feebly tried to teach them agriculture. Few citizens sympathized, and fewer helped. Instead the whites taught them property, and then how to convey it under the constitutional treaty clause. Presidents Jefferson and Madison negotiated fifty-three cession treaties, degrading the tribes from protectorates to wards, while acquiring tens of millions of acres for which the fictitiously sovereign nations received annuities to keep them in rags and drunken idleness.[27]

Blacks fared even worse. In their precursory publication, *American Slavery As It Is* of 1839, Theodore Weld and his wife, Angelina Grimké, spoke for the African-American slave, providing the public documentary evidence of appalling cruelties:

We will prove that the slaves in the United States are treated with barbarous inhumanity; that they are overworked, underfed, wretchedly clad and lodged, and have insufficient sleep; that they are often made to wear round their necks iron collars armed with prongs, to drag heavy chains and weights at their feet while working in the field, and to wear yokes, and bells, and iron horns . . . that they are often hunted with bloodhounds and shot down like beasts, or torn in pieces by dogs; that they are often suspended by the arms and whipped and beaten till they faint, and when revived by restoratives, beaten again till they faint, and sometimes till they die; that their ears are often cut off, their eyes knocked out, their bones broken, their flesh branded with red hot irons; that they are maimed, mutilated, and burned to death over slow fires. All these things, and more, and worse, we shall *prove*. Reader, we know whereof we affirm, we have weighed it well; *more and worse* WE WILL PROVE.[28]

Oppression of the black man continued, as we know, even after emancipation, inexorably establishing two societies, one comparatively privileged, the other deprived, developing an insidious pattern of segregation that was profoundly to affect urban life and settlement policies through to modern times.

The decade of the 1830s was one of wild land speculation. Chicago was still prairie in 1833. Then it boomed. According to Tunnard and Reed, land was bought and sold and lots staked out for a population of one million. A parcel could change hands ten times a day. Jumps in price resulted from a precarious sales system that returned the land to the original owner when the bottom dropped out of the market. By 1856, Chicago was a fully developed city of almost 100,000, the focus of ten railroad trunk lines, and a classic example of the artless, commercial grid.

Before 1850 America's energy source was water, and water bodies provided long-distance travel routes as well. Although muddy streets were common, the air in water mill towns was pure. But the new source of power, steam, voraciously devoured coal and changed everything. The American novelist Rebecca Harding Davis describes a typical iron mill town of the late 1850s, Wheeling, West Virginia:

The idiosyncracy of this town is smoke. It rolls sullenly in slow folds from the great chimneys of the iron foundries and settles down in black, slimy pools on the muddy streets. Smoke on the wharves, smoke on the dingy boats, on the yellow river,—clinging in a coating of greasy soot to the housefront, the two faded poplars, the faces of the passers-by. The long train of mules, dragging masses of pig-iron through the narrow street, have a foul vapour hanging to their reeking sides.[29]

The Industrial Revolution was begun. In the 1850s the United States provided perfect capitalistic conditions: a huge domestic market, tariff barriers, an extensive transportation system, many inventions in industrial machinery, abundant natural resources, a large labor force, domestic and foreign capital, and a laissez-faire government. Business structure also changed from predominantly private ownership to corporations, preparing the groundwork for the later monopolistic control of many industries.

The railroad took over as the major form of transportation, eventually displacing canals. Within cities the railroads got permission to go wherever they wished by bribing councilmen and aldermen, cutting some cities into jigsaw puzzles. Between cities, the railroad appropriated the beautiful shores of rivers and lakes, employing a similar system of acquisition.

Where greed knows no bounds no offer is generous enough, no appetite adequately satiated. The story of the transcontinental railroads makes this point superbly. In a charter granted by Congress in 1862, the Union Pacific Railroad was retained to construct a railroad from Nebraska to California. The agreement gave the promoters of the company (1) a right of way, (2) twenty "sections" of government land (twenty square miles: the size of Manhattan) for every mile of track constructed, and (3) free use of minerals and timber on the public lands. In addition to these enormously generous grants, the U.S. government agreed to equally generous loans to the company: $16,000 for every mile built across the plains, and across the plateaus and mountains, $32,000 and $48,000, respectively. A California corporation, the Central Pacific Railroad, was granted similar terms to build a line eastward to meet the Union Pacific. A member of the California Constitutional Convention in 1879 gave the following account of the blackmailing tactics of the Central Pacific Railroad:

They start out their railway track and survey their line near a thriving village. They go to the most prominent citizens of that village and say, "If you will give us so many thousand dollars we will run through here; if you do not we will run by," and in every instance where the subsidy was not granted, that course was taken, and the effect was just as they said, to kill off the little town. Here was the town of Paradise in Stanislaus County; because they did not get what they wanted, they established another town four miles from there. In every instance where they were refused a subsidy, in money, unless their terms were acceded to, they have established a depot near to the place and always have frozen them out.[30]

After the Civil War, the South had to change. Slave labor was over. Farms and plantations were in ruins. Between 1865 and 1869 carpetbagger state governments manipulated the black vote throughout the South. As a result, blacks began to enter the mainstream. But in the early 1870s, the Ku Klux Klan and other secret societies used terrorism and brutality to regain white supremacy. As a result, many blacks were afraid to vote. By 1872 thousands of former confederates retrieved their political privileges and destroyed carpet-bagger state governments.

Cheap farm labor was thus regained. Blacks were kept from the election polls by intimidation, kept from skilled jobs by poor education, and kept at their old station by a pervasive campaign of racism and ridicule. By 1877, white control was fully reinstated in the South. Aided by railroad networks, southern industrialization and urbanization slowly began to develop.

In the North towns vied for population to attract industries, which in turn attracted huge populations of foreign workers. European immigration skyrocketed between 1840 and 1910, from about 600,000 in the decade 1831-40, to over 5 million in the decade 1881-90. Between 1860 and 1900 America's urban population quadrupled. (The all-time high of 8.8 million immigrants occurred in the decade 1901-10.) Many immigrants were imported to work in coal mines and steel mills in or near Pittsburgh, Pennsylvania, living and working under conditions of egregious squalor. Poles, Austrians, Hungarians, Slavs, and Italians subsisted there on the smallest quantities of food, worked under incredible dangers of one fatal accident a day (if they worked at all), resided in hideous living quarters, working twelve or more hours a day, six days a week, even as children in many cases. An employer, when confronted with his workers' agonizing circumstances, protested: "They don't suffer; why, they can't even speak English!" Labor unions were outlawed in those days and the supremely prosperous industrial employers made all decisions having to do with wages, hours, and safety measures. Unemployment was extremely high, and any kind of work under any kind of conditions was considered better than none at all. Children shared in this hell on earth; 26 percent of all boys between the ages of ten and fifteen were employed in 1900. Employed children were especially prey to the maiming and fatal accidents that resulted from their aching fatigue.

In describing the working conditions of the steel town of McKeesport, Pennsylvania, a Hungarian churchman wrote:

Thousands of immigrants wander here from year to year . . . and here they suffer till they are swallowed up in the inferno. . . .

Scarce an hour passes without an accident, and no day without a
fatal disease. But what if *one* man be crippled, if *one* life be extin-
guished among so many! Each place can be filled from *ten* men, all
eager for it. Newcomers camp out within sight of the factory gates,
while a little farther away, others arrive with almost daily regular-
ity — thousands of immigrants to don the fetters of slavery.[31]

Industrialists enriched themselves almost beyond description in this
period. For example, in 1900 Andrew Carnegie's income from his steel
company alone, tax free, was twenty thousand times greater than that of
the average worker. The inclusion of Carnegie's income from properties
and investment would shoot this dizzying figure even higher. Much of the
wealth of this period was squandered on trivia in feverish orgies of com-
petitive spending. A hilarious example is an elaborate banquet on horse-
back. Every guest was mounted on a horse and lavishly served a twelve-
course dinner in this position. To some degree the English philosopher,
Herbert Spencer, was behind this virtual crushing of the have-nots, this
near enslavement that produced such millions of dollars.

> In the 1860s [Herbert Spencer] applied Darwin's biological concept
> of the survival of the fittest to Man and created a science of society.
> "Light came as in a flood and all was clear," exclaimed Andrew
> Carnegie on first reading Spencer's work. Americans in all walks of
> life . . . wholeheartedly accepted the notion that free and even
> violent competition among individuals was essential to the natural
> rise of the fittest who were destined to lead America. Only a few
> found any contradiction in the fact that these business leaders, in the
> name of economic freedom, were organizing the national economy
> into giant combines, monopolies and trusts. . . . Americans em-
> braced the ideal of "bigness" as they embraced the ideals of free
> competition and the survival of the fittest—in the corporation, in
> wealth, in the labor force, in social problems and in their cities.
> Little wonder that they created hideous industrial towns and giant
> jungle cities, instruments at once of pride and despair.[32]

In 1894 the workers of the Pullman Palace Car Company went on an
illegal strike. This story, vividly told in Irving Stone's *Clarence Darrow
for the Defense*, is an excellent example of the vise that workers were
placed in by ruthless industrialists. Every worker had to live in the company town. But in the depression year of 1893 Pullman cut wages from
$3.20 a day to $1.20 a day without cutting rents, fraudulently claiming
that the rental company was not under his control. This $1.20 a day wage
covered rent and nothing else. As the workers, along with their families,
were therefore facing starvation, they had no choice but to strike. During

the subsequent U.S. Senate investigation, it was discovered that Pullman's profit dividend during the year of cut wages was $2.8 million, plus cash profits in the company treasury of $26 million, in addition to $36 million in invested capital. If Pullman had taken a mere $100,000 from profit dividends, or 1/28th of the year's profits, and left it in the workingmen's wages, all that misery could have been avoided. Pullman's comment during the Senate investigation was that his duty was to stockholders and his company, and there was "no reason to give those workingmen a gift of money."[33]

Such floods of immigration would almost automatically create intolerable residential overcrowding. Slightly more than half of Manhattan's 1870 population of 942,292 lived in the area between 14th Street and City Hall. Density on the Lower East Side in 1890 for the tenement house population of immigrants, desperate for employment, reached 290,000 persons per square mile, and this represents a density that has never since been equaled anywhere on earth, including the Far East. Jacob Riis reported that one five-story tenement on Crosby Street contained 101 adults and 91 children. The death rate in these tenements was extremely high, sanitation being almost impossible to maintain.

The dumbbell tenement was introduced in New York in 1879 as an "improvement" over the previous tenement (ironically); it was not as deep, with more windows on air shafts (creating a dumbbell shape in plan), and a ground coverage of only 65 percent. Dumbbell tenements in turn were banned around 1900, although hundreds, perhaps thousands, still stand to this day.

In tandem with the excesses of the Industrial Revolution ran those of municipal corruption, beginning in 1857 with New York's Tweed Ring of criminal municipal officials. William Marcy Tweed, leader of the Tammany Political Machine, effected a system of graft through construction contract kickbacks and other means that lasted until 1871, when he was finally brought down by reformers. During Tweed's time in power the ring stole between $30 and $200 million. The Viaduct Plan for the construction of the elevated railroad on New York's major streets and avenues was a Tweed Ring project. A colossal opportunity for graft, the "El" caused a tumultuous degradation of urban life. Families living in tenements closely bordering the tracks had no choice but to experience, every five or ten minutes, the El's roaring, screeching, clatter, and vibration. Until electrified in 1900, coal smoke and cinders poured into the windows and ashes fell on pedestrians below. Profiting from all of New York's public development in his day, Tweed held up construction of the Brooklyn Bridge until someone brought him a carpet bag containing $60,000 in cash earmarked for the board of aldermen. Nothing was on the cuff.

From 1865 to about 1910 municipal corruption was the order of the day in American cities. The nobility of public service had been replaced by the reality of political machines that arrogantly treated municipal govern-ments as businesses. The indifference shown by the general public was astounding.

Through his 1902-3 articles in *McClure's Magazine* the great muck-raker Lincoln Steffens exposed the wild municipal corruption of the past thirty years and continuing, in St. Louis, Minneapolis, Pittsburgh, Phil-adelphia, and Chicago.[34] City fathers, whether councilmen, aldermen, or mayors, managed to turn their city governments into highly profitable businesses. In one city the municipal assemblymen had a bribery price list: so much for a grain elevator, so much for a street improvement, a franchise, or a public contract. Typically, boodlers would "control" saloons, gambling houses, and bordellos by outlawing them except at certain times and places, then doubling all the prices and taking half. Pittsburgh was different. Boodlers *became* the law through a careful process of council and legislature ownership. All interfering laws were changed to favor their interests. Two or three men ruled Pittsburgh between 1870 and 1903, and perhaps longer. In some cities municipal affairs somehow continued to function; in others they eventually ground to a halt. In the end Steffens found: "In all cities the better classes—the business men—are the sources of corruption.[35] Moreover, when citizens are "too busy for self-government," their city government is ripe for takeover by clever and greedy criminals.[36]

Oliver McClintock, in an 1896 paper read before the municipal organi-zation attempting to fight the stranglehold on Pittsburgh by boodlers, stated that he had found prominent merchants, contractors, manufac-turers, wealthy capitalists, and bankers all against reform:

> In still another direction we found that the financial and political sup-port of the great steam railroads and largest manufacturing corpo-rations, controlling as far as they were able the suffrages of their thou-sands of employees, were thrown against us, for the simple reason, as was frankly explained by one of them, that it was much easier to deal with a boss in promoting their corporate interests than to deal directly with the people's representatives in the municipal legislature.[37]

H. L. Mencken's convulsive description of the residential buildings in Pennsylvania's Westmoreland Valley cries out to be reproduced here, at least in part. (Every vivid sentence could be italicized):

> On a Winter day some years ago, coming out of Pittsburgh on one of the expresses of the Pennsylvania Railroad, I rolled eastward for an hour through the coal and steel towns of Westmoreland country. It was familiar ground; boy and man, I had been through it often before. But somehow I had never quite sensed its appalling desola-

tion. Here was the very heart of industrial America, the center of its most lucrative and characteristic activity, the boast and pride of the richest and grandest nation ever seen on earth—and here was a scene so dreadfully hideous, so intolerably bleak and forlorn that it reduced the whole aspiration of man to a macabre and depressing joke. Here was wealth beyond computation, almost beyond imagination—and here were human habitations so abominable that they would have disgraced a race of alley cats.

I am not speaking of mere filth. One expects steel towns to be dirty. What I allude to is the unbroken and agonizing ugliness, the sheer revolting monstrousness, of every house in sight. From East Liberty to Greensburg, a distance of twenty-five miles, there was not one in sight from the train that did not insult and lacerate the eye. Some were so bad, and they were among the most pretentious—churches, stores, warehouses, and the like—that they were downright startling; one blinked before them as one blinks before a man with his face shot away. . . . There was not a single decent house within eye-range from the Pittsburgh suburbs to the Greensburg yards. There was not one that was not misshapen, and there was not one that was not shabby.

The country itself is not uncomely, despite the grime of the endless mills. . . . Nearly every house, big and little, has space on all four sides. Obviously, if there were architects of any professional sense or dignity in the region, they would have perfected a chalet to hug the hillsides . . . a low and clinging building, wider than it was tall. But what have they done? They have taken as their model a brick set on end. This they have converted into a thing of dingy clapboards, with a narrow, low-pitched roof. And the whole they have set upon thin, preposterous brick piers. By the hundreds and thousands these abominable houses cover the bare hillsides, like gravestones in some gigantic and decaying cemetery. On their deep sides they are three, four and even five stories high; on their low sides they bury themselves swinishly in the mud. Not a fifth of them are perpendicular. They lean this way and that, hanging onto their bases precariously. And one and all they are streaked in grime, with dead and eczematous patches of paint peeping through the streaks.[38]

Poets and novelists of the late nineteenth century had a variety of reactions to major American cities. Theodore Dreiser, novelist and spokesman for the have-nots of the period, felt "intense sympathy" for the "helpless degradation" of the poor, the brutalities they were "compelled to endure." Yet on a personal level he loved cities for all their brutality. He praised the Chicago of the 1880s for characteristics others deplored: stockyards, steel works, squalid shanties, can-strewn yards, grinding wheels, brawlers, prostitutes, and slatterns. "I liked the life. I was crazy about it. Chicago was like a great orchestra in a tumult of noble harmonies. I was like a guest at a feast, eating and drinking in a delirium of ecstasy."[39]

As a newcomer to New York in the 1890s, Dreiser, not surprisingly, admired its gluttony and power: "Here, as one could feel, were huge dreams and lust and vanities being gratified hourly. I wanted to know the worst and the best of it."[40] Unable to find work as a reporter, however, he became jaded:

> There was that astounding contrast between wealth and poverty, here more sharply emphasized than anywhere else in America, which gave the great city a gross and cruel and mechanical look . . . a look so harsh and indifferent at times as to leave me a little numb. . . . New York was difficult and revolting. The police and politicians were a menace; vice was rampant; wealth was shamelessly showy, cold and brutal. In New York the outsider or beginner had scarcely any chance at all save as a servant. The city was overrun with hungry, loafing men of all descriptions, newspaper writers included.[41]

Edith Wharton found the New York of the 1870s intolerably ugly. She deplored "its untouched streets and the narrow houses so lacking in external dignity," its "deadly uniformity of mean ugliness," the "cramped horizontal gridiron of a town without towers, porticoes, fountains or perspectives . . . and the city's mean monotonous streets, without architecture, without great churches or palaces, or any visible memorials of an historic past."[42]

Walt Whitman, however, in a letter of October 9, 1868, conveys what probably was then, and still is, New York's greatest attraction—the excitement and electricity of its streets and sidewalks, the unceasing panorama of assertive human life:

> It is a never-ending amusement and study and recreation for me to ride a couple of hours on a pleasant afternoon on a Broadway stage in this way. You see everything as you pass, a sort of living, endless panorama—shops and splendid buildings and great windows: on the broad sidewalks crowds of women richly dressed continually passing, altogether different, superior in style and looks from any to be seen anywhere else—in fact a perfect stream of people—men too dressed in high style, and plenty of foreigners—and then in the streets the thick crowd of carriages, stages, carts, hotel and private coaches, and in fact all sorts of vehicles and many first-class teams, mile after mile, and the splendor of such a great street and so many tall, ornamental, noble buildings many of them of white marble, and the gayety and motion on every side.[43]

Another great American novelist, Henry James, left America in 1876 to reside in London, principally because of his dislike of American cities. James found American cities wanting in terms of relaxed and refined conversation and historic association. He referred to "the colossal greed of New York," and charged that the millionaire was virtually the city's sole god. And although he found New York exhilarating, it was not enough to outweigh its disadvantages. Looked at from the river, he saw New York with its tall buildings (even at that time) as a "pin-cushion in profile"![44]

> [The buildings] never begin to speak to you in the manner of the builded majesties of the world . . . towers or temples or fortresses or palaces—with the authority of things of permanence or even of things of long duration. . . . The great city is projected into its future as, practically, a huge, continuous fifty-floored conspiracy against the very idea of the ancient graces.[45]

To James, Washington was the only city in America that had civilizing qualities, a "City of Conversation" in which topics were adorned with "ingenuity and humour," in which the world of business was given no value.[46] Also grieving, Henry Adams found that "the world after 1865 became a banker's world."[47] He was particularly critical of Boston: "There is no society worth the name, no wit, no intellectual energy or competition, no clash of minds or schools, no interests, no masculine self-assertion or ambition. . . . Boston is running dry of literary authorities."[48]

One could make a case for the proposition that by 1880 Hamilton's oligarchical capitalism and the ultimate excesses of the Industrial Revolution—cruel extremes of wealth and poverty and pervasive corruption of city governments—had all but obliterated within ninety years the cultural, intellecual, and social-reformative qualities of American cities— qualities great world cities had fostered for centuries.

Today's eastern and midwestern cities bear the imprint of earlier centuries. Streets have been closed and added of course, but overall street patterns became fixed, once established. In addition, because of the cost of demolition, original constructions have remained in place, unless highly favorable new-construction profits were projected, or unless government-financed urban redevelopment became a major part of the financial picture. Industries and institutions abandon in-town structures after moving to new outlying locations. Until such a property is considered profitable by a new occupant or developer, its structure stands empty. In towns in which the new-housing market is weak, in-city houses are variously maintained, rehabilitated, or converted to apartments or (oddly) to retail. They can also be abandoned. By and large, only a strong market for new accommodations brings new development to an already developed site. Needless to say, in prime sections of major cities that strong market seems to be ever-present. (In fact, in prime sections the

problem has been too much redevelopment, causing the wholesale elimination of seventeenth- and eighteenth-century architecture and land-
marks.) In small and middle-sized older cities, however, most of the existing development dates back to the sixty-year period between 1870 and
1930. Thus roughly half, if not more, of the deplorable parts of today's
American cities were already in place by 1900, and another 10 to 20 percent were built by 1930.

The first dozen years of the twentieth century saw the construction of
civic art in abundance—state capitols, railroad terminals, numerous
public structures designed in the Beaux Arts classical manner. This brief
but magnificent era of the City Beautiful is discussed in the next chapter.

In the first third of the twentieth century the power of the industrial
moguls was restricted somewhat by antitrust actions and income tax legislation. The early decades saw great labor struggles, resulting in a significant shift of power toward labor unions. This shift ultimately brought
about the introduction of a new market of working-class homeowners.
Increased wages made the dream of a suburban house, with its lush green
lawn, within financial reach and made the purchase of a private car both
a possibility and a necessity.

U.S. population almost tripled between 1900 and 1980. Urban population grew intensely through 1950, as fewer and fewer workers were
needed for agriculture. The suburban outflux of middle-income families
is the undoubted cause of a dip in the populations of many cities between
1950 and 1980. Largely because of in-migration from other parts of the
nation, Sunbelt cities experienced significant population increases in the
decade between 1970 and 1980.

The automobile played an extraordinary part in America's twentieth-
century development. Car ownership sprang from 77,400 in 1905 to over
23 million in 1930.[49] By 1988 that figure had reached over 140 million.[50]

Parkways were introduced early in the century to allow people to enjoy
nature, as they left the city behind for a day. After World War II, speed
became the objective and the elimination of those annoying grade
crossings that required so many stops. Enter thruways, turnpikes, expressways, and freeways: limited-access highways that carried trucks as well as
private cars. This movement was culminated in the postwar Interstate
Highway Program, awesome in scope, that linked virtually every part of
the nation, even wilderness and farm areas that will never again be
entirely peaceful. Early portions of the interstate program obliterated
whole neighborhoods, paid no relocation costs, and fractured old cities
with elevated highways. By the time the program was virtually complete
in the 1970s, community participation and environmental impact statements were part of the land-acquisition and route-designation procedure.
By and large, however, opposition groups merely postponed the inevitable. Here was a case of absolute and perfect market demand, for the
human being loves its car as it loves sex, perhaps more. The "rubber

lobby," consisting of industries dealing with motor-vehicular products, faced little opposition in Congress, as the Interstate Highway Program was allowed to slaughter cargo railroads, ultimately eliminating unsubsidized passenger railroads, as well. Even more astounding, rubber lobby members criminally destroyed electric transit in some cities, as described in Chapter 9.

The vast migration of rural southerners, largely black, to northern and southern cities between 1933 and 1945 was caused in part by the Agricultural Adjustment Act of 1933. This was President Franklin Roosevelt's well-intentioned attempt to solve the problem of surplus production of cotton. But the management of the act was sabotaged by its rogue administrator, Chester Davis, who let the plantation owners keep each subsidy payment in its entirety and remove the tenant farmers, according to Fligstein. This was the reverse of the act's intention. Thousands of tenant farmers were forced off the land. In addition, this infusion of subverted capital permitted plantation owners to buy labor-saving machines, further reducing the need for manpower in cotton production. Booming war industries in both southern and northern cities at least gave former tenant farmers employment. Following World War II far too many unskilled poor people were induced to migrate to these cities, in wave after wave of migration, long after employment rolls were filled. The obvious result was overcrowding, unemployment, and public dependence at a time when skilled jobs began to be on the increase and unskilled jobs were dwindling. This employment trend has, of course, continued to this day and promises to grow ever larger.

Just as the postwar migration to northern cities was getting into high gear, the Veterans Administration (VA) was authorized to offer home mortgages to war veterans at a mere 4 percent. Two-family houses were not eligible, town houses were not eligible. The home had to be for one family and detached. Whether by design or by mistake, the VA's detached-house proviso turned out to be a major instigator in the migration of middle-income families, mostly white, to the suburbs of American cities: *the great outflux*. And as the middle-income group moved out, the poor, white and nonwhite, moved in. This in turn had its own powerful effect, and the educational standards of the urban public schools somehow declined significantly.

Racism spurred this outflux, but this was not the whole story. A powerful truth was demonstrated: middle-income parents will do anything to give their children a good educational start in life. If moving out of the city is the only affordable way to do it, they will move out of the city, even if this goes against their adult lifestyle preferences. Middle-income blacks were kept out of most suburban areas through the segregation policies of real estate brokers. In time, however, certain villages became in effect black suburbs.

Thus despite federal assistance to cities since World War II, by and large the white middle-income group and a portion of the black have left the inner cities of America. Although the outflux was started by the postwar VA mortgages, the undesirable conditions in the urban schools, sometimes deplorable, had everything to do with its perpetuation. Today many northern cities have proportions of poor people entirely too high for good municipal health, with only a smattering of the remaining middle-income families sending their children to public schools. The result of this spiral has been the deterioration of many American cities.

Low-income public housing was introduced in 1937 and has produced relatively few housing units in relation to the need (about 1.3 million nationwide by 1985.) The massive structural design employed for public housing in large cities has frequently caused a furor. Since that time various mortgage programs to encourage private development of low- and moderate-income housing have been introduced by liberal congresses and eventually killed by conservative ones—cancelled long before the housing needs of these groups were even approached.

VA mortgages sparked another twentieth-century developmental phenomenon, the fully-developed speculative subdivision, each as large as an entire village. Levittown, New York, built in the late 1940s, was one of the first such communities of single-family detached houses. It offered homebuyers a half-dozen or so design variations and other improvements over the horrendous look-alike subdivisions of prior decades in which no tree was left standing and no house differed from the rest, in which streets were mercilously gridded, and in which mechanization took command of the homestead.

In Fairfax County, Virginia, just southwest of Washington, D.C., immense portions of land area remained undeveloped before World War II. After the war it was developed in a little more than a decade. Here, as in other postwar counties, better-designed speculative housing created new single-family neighborhoods, as did the old mechanized look-alike kind. Parkways, highways, and expressways took everyone to the capital. Lesser highways took inhabitants to small convenience shopping centers, where huge pedestalled signs all but grabbed each passing car and deposited its contents of potential customers into the designated store. Taking a leaf from the ugliest of gas stations, each sign was built larger, stood higher, and glowed brighter than the erection just in front. The result was a vast headache of structural slurb.

The outlying shopping center or mall has been as ruinous to American cities as the outflux of the middle-income group. Introduced after World War II, it contained one or more department stores, and it siphoned off most of the retail trade from the downtown of the nearby city. It is still in full sway and multiplying. The shopping mall is responsible for a loss of feeling of community and the sense of place that downtowns provide. Moreover, chain stores can afford shopping mall rents, while beginning or striving enterprises cannot. The result is a glitzy sameness, mall after mall. Despite a few successful efforts to build shopping malls within urban downtowns and to redesign downtowns with the desirable features of shopping centers—ease of approach, ease of parking, safe pedestrian circulation, cheerful and attractive amenities—the downtowns of many middle-sized and small cities have become doomed. Some struggle to their feet when a downtown improvement committee sparks a revitalization plan, only to be slapped down again when still another outlying shopping mall springs up.

A few consultant planners contributed to the doom. They wrote books and pamphlets on good shopping center design when the tragedy was the very existence of the outlying shopping center and the draining off of the city's commercial nucleus.

Without commerce, a city cannot endure. Without a middle class, a city cannot endure, and too many American "cities" are merely urban places today, places that function ony in part, at times, and in certain quarters.

What is acutely sad about the demise of downtowns is that preventive measures were conceivable. Legal steps could have been taken to restrict the proliferation of shopping malls on virgin soil and to provide all their advantages in existing downtowns. The same could be said of urban schools: workable improvements could have made them first rate. These two killers have been loose in our cities and towns for more than forty years, and in effect we just stand by and watch.

European cities still have thriving downtowns, to which millions of American travelers, among others, can attest. Democratic Europeans take planning seriously. I think it is safe to say that no developer would be permitted to create a shopping center or mall capable of economically ruining a nearby downtown. European planning is discussed more fully in Chapter 10.

The twentieth century's vast increases in urban population have produced ever greater increases in land value and ever greater enthusiasm for speculative gambling in American urban land. Where the city is not dying, the urban problem is overdevelopment: overdevelopment in cities and towns where every unbuilt parcel is considered a real estate bonanza, overdevelopment that encroaches on treasured wilderness and pastoral areas, overdevelopment in terms of ever-extruding building height in existing cities. Money, profits, bottom line—no thought given to nature, sunlight, community, or order unless the profits are immense.

NOTES

1. Chief Luther Standing Bear of the Oglala Band of the Sioux, quoted in T. C. McLuhan, *Touch the Earth. A Self-Portrait of Indian Existence* (New York: Promentory Press, 1971), p. 45.

2. Holy Wintu woman, quoted in ibid., p. 15.

3. John Adams (second president of the United States), quoted in Harold Underwood Faulkner and Tyler Kepner, *America, Its History and People* (New York: Harper & Brothers, 1938), p. 90.

4. *Webster's Guide to American History* (Springfield, Mass.: G. & C. Merriam Company, 1971), p. 66.

5. Central Park from 59th Street to approximately 99th Street.

6. Merrill D. Peterson, "Thomas Jefferson: A Brief Life," in *Thomas Jefferson, The Man . . . His World . . . His Influence,* ed. Lally Weymouth (New York: G. P. Putnam's Sons, 1973), p. 23.

7. John W. Reps, *The Making of Urban America* (Princeton, N.J.: Princeton University Press, 1965), pp. 216-17.

8. Faulkner and Kepner, *America, Its History and People*, p. 113.

9. Ibid.

10. Ibid., p. 108.

11. John C. Miller, *Alexander Hamilton: Portrait in Paradox* (New York: Harper & Brothers, 1959), p. 233.

12. Ibid., p. 240.

13. Ibid., p. 243.

14. Historians and biographers differ as to whether Jefferson and Madison, or Hamilton, proffered the proposal, but among those consulted, those who point to the Virginians in this respect are the more persuasive.

15. Miller, p. 250; Broadus Mitchell, *Alexander Hamilton, The National Adventure, 1788-1804* (New York: The MacMillan Company, 1962), p. 83; and Merrill D. Peterson, *Thomas Jefferson and the New Nation* (New York: Oxford University Press, 1970), p. 413.

16. Peterson, *Thomas Jefferson and the New Nation*, p. 413.

17. J. W. Moulton, *New York 170 Years Ago* (New York: 1843) quoted in Rudofsky, *Streets for People* (Garden City, N.Y.: Doubleday & Company, Inc., 1964), p. 25.

18. Bernard Rudofsky, *Streets for People* (Garden City, N.Y.: Doubleday & Company, Inc., 1964), p. 29.

19. Reps, p. 299 (The Commissioners' Plan is quoted).

20. Edgar Allan Poe, *Doings of Gotham*, collected by Jacob E. Spannuth (Pottsville, Penn.: Jacob E. Spannuth, Publishers, 1929), pp. 25-26, 40-41. (Letters addressed to Eli Bowen of the *Columbia Spy* of Columbia, Penn.)

21. Christopher Tunnard and Henry Hope Reed, *American Skyline* (New York: Mentor Books, 1956), pp. 20-21.

22. Lewis Mumford, *The City in History* (New York: Harcourt Brace & World, Inc., 1961), p. 422.

23. Ibid., p. 423.

24. Ibid., p. 418.

25. Ibid., p. 423-24.

26. Ibid., p. 444.

27. Marshall Smelser, *The Democratic Republic, 1801-1815* (New York: Harper & Row, 1968), pp. 132-34.

28. Theodore Weld and Angelina Grimké, *American Slavery As It Is*, 1839. Reprinted: (New York: Arno Press and The New York Times, 1968), p. 9.

29. Rebecca Harding Davis, *Atlantic Tales* (Boston: Ticknor & Fields, 1866), p. 50.

30. Glenn Chesney Quiett, *They Built the West: An Epic of Rails and Cities* (New York: D. Appleton-Century Co., Inc., 1934), p. 83.

31. Frederick Lewis Allen, *The Big Change* (New York: Harper & Brothers, 1952), pp. 58-59.

32. Tunnard and Reed, *American Skyline*, p. 118.

33. Irving Stone, *Clarence Darrow for the Defense* (New York: Bantam Books, 1965), p. 29.

34. Lincoln Steffens, *The Shame of the Cities* (New York: Hill & Wang, Inc., 1957). These articles, compiled in one volume, were originally published in 1904 by S. D. McClure, Phillips & Company.

35. Ibid., p. 40.

36. Ibid., p. 105.

37. Ibid., p. 126.

38. Mencken, *Prejudices, Sixth Series*, pp. 187-88. Although Mencken's trip occurred in the early twentieth century, these constructions clearly owe their inception to the Industrial Revolution.

39. Theodore Dreiser, *A Book About Myself* (New York: Boni & Liveright, 1922), pp. 20, 107.

40. Ibid., p. 452.

41. Ibid., pp. 452, 482, 487.

42. Edith Wharton, *A Backward Glance* (New York: D. Appleton-Century Co., Inc., 1934), pp. 54-55.

43. Walt Whitman, Letter to "Pete," quoted in William James, *Talks to Teachers on Psychology and to Students on Some of Life's Ideals* (New York: Henry Holt Company, 1899), pp. 251-52.

44. Henry James, *American Scene*, ed. W. H. Auden (New York: Charles Scribner's Sons, 1946), pp. 76, 342.

45. Ibid., pp. 77, 92.

46. Ibid., pp. 342-43.

47. Henry Adams, *Education of Henry Adams* (Boston: Houghton Mifflin Company, 1918), p. 247.

48. Henry Adams, *Letters of Henry Adams, 1858-1891*, ed. W. C. Ford (Boston: Houghton Mifflin Company, 1930), pp. 228, 288.

49. U.S. Department of Commerce, Bureau of the Census, *Historical Statistics of the United States, Colonial Times to 1970* (Washington, D.C., 1975), p. 716.

50. U.S. Department of Commerce, Bureau of the Census, *Statistical Abstract of the United States, 1990*, 110th Edition (Washington, D.C., 1990), Table 1028.

3

Survey of American City Planning
City Planning's Ability to Meet the Challenge

City planning has thus been preceded in America by extensive free and unplanned urban development and is still overwhelmed, if not engulfed, by it. This chapter gives an overview of the efforts of American planning to stem or correct economic and developmental devastation.

While it is true that the laying out of streets is but one phase of city planning, it is an important one. Obviously a city must be built around designated channels of movement, and its street layout markedly affects everything that follows. As we have seen, virtually all attempts at grandeur had to give way to the speculative gridiron plan. Numerous American street layouts of the seventeenth and eighteenth centuries, grand as well as ordinary, are chronicled and illustrated in Reps, *The Making of Urban America*. Tunnard and Reed's *American Skyline* also expands on this subject.[1]

The American city planning movement did not actually start until the late nineteenth century, but two early approaches to the ideal human community bear mentioning. The first consisted of the *sectarian and nonsectarian experimental communities* founded in the eighteenth and early nineteenth centuries. Occurring in every size and variety, each group sought to create, in this vast land of opportunity, its own heaven on earth. Religious communities included Oneida, New York, which lasted about thirty years, Economy, Pennsylvania, seventy-five years, and Bethlehem, Pennsylvania and Salt Lake City which still exist. While more than one hundred experimental communities were started in America, involving over 100,000 people, the nonsectarian versions lasted only two years on average. Not surprisingly, the developmental patterns of these towns failed to reflect the richness and variety of the founders' ideals and principles.

Although wildly optimistic hearts thus attempted to establish perfect societies, every community that failed seems to have had a fatal flaw in its grand scheme. For example, Robert Owens' community, New Harmony, Indiana, was excessively patriarchal, while the Oneida Community in New York prohibited marriage (procreation was organized by the elders.) The Shaker colony, Watervliet, New York, required celibacy. It is difficult to conceive (sorry) of a totally celibate society continuing indefintely.

> Although these groups were numerous, their influence on American society was modest. The bulk of the nation stubbornly pursued its old sinful and capitalistic ways. . . . Their neighbors viewed these sects and their leaders either with outright hostility or with the pity usually reserved for the dim-witted or the helpless.
>
> The physical impact of the utopians was equally slight. With the exception of the Mormons no one of these groups made any significant impression on the pattern of towns in its region. Perhaps this is why we value all the more such artifacts as may have survived in a Bethlehem, a New Harmony, or an Amana.
>
> If the heritage of bricks and mortar is meager, the utopians at least left a rich legacy of hopes and dreams. One should not be too harsh in judging what, with the advantage of a lengthened perspective, now appears as ludicrous or wildly impractical schemes to reconstruct society. The modern city planner, who himself must be something of a utopian if he is to maintain his idealism and sanity in an increasingly ugly and chaotic world, may appear equally absurd a century hence.[2]

The second early approach to the ideal community was systematic rather than structural. In the late nineteenth and early twentieth centuries a considerable number of *narrative utopias* were conceived and published in England and America, undoubtedly in reactive revulsion to the widespread cruelties of the Industrial Revolution. For example, *Looking Backward* by the American Edward Bellamy was published in 1888. Although *A Modern Utopia* was written by an Englishman, H. G. Wells, in 1905, his concept addressed the entire western world.[3]

The utopian fabricator had a tendency toward naiveté with respect to sin and human nature. He seems to have imagined that vice, crime, greed, and lust for power would be unknown if basic needs were universally met. (Bellamy even believed that the absence of crime precluded the need for lawyers!)

These narrative utopias demonstrate that even the most exalted of human spirits harbors a little despotism. For example, Bellamy's political regime is run exclusively by men past the age of 45. Women have certain economic advantages but are served only by a separate women's political regime. H. G. Wells' system removes all criminals to various islands in the Atlantic where they are permitted to organize their own communities and practice crime upon each other. Oddly enough for a democratic socialist's conception, Wells' scheme had another quality that one might well view as repressive: every individual would be required to register with the government his name, number, and fingerprints. Each citizen's changed social statistics, if any, would be reported to the government with regimental promptness.

Despite these faults, utopian thinkers at least attempted to come to grips with all the needs of a society instead of confining themselves to currently pressing issues. This cannot be said of the city planning profession, which as conveyed on succeeding pages, addresses only historically allocated urban subjects.

The American city planning movement was officially launched in 1893 on the heels of the magnificent Chicago World's Fair (World's Columbian Exposition.) The principal figures were Frederick Law Olmstead, a landscape architect, and Daniel Burnham, an architect. In the twenty-five years prior to that date a few new towns, actually suburbs, had been constructed, and urban reforms had been initiated dealing with health, sanitation, and housing, but these were scattered, single-issue campaigns. Independently, and quite miraculously, Congress passed in 1893 the Tarnsey Act, which authorized the federal government to assist in the financing of major public buildings in cities all over the country. The construction of monumental post offices and customs houses was followed by magnificent new state capitols and city halls, railroad terminals, civic centers, art museums, park systems, and university campuses. The best architects were retained: Cass Gilbert, McKim, Mead and White, and Calvert Vaux, among others. Civic adornment reigned supreme. The name of the age was the City Beautiful.

It is fortunate for America that these components came together as they did, for without the City Beautiful movement, the nation would today have few of the monumental buildings its people treasure and try to hold onto—fabulous beaux arts structures that need not tower to be commanding.

In this period Burnham and Olmstead separately prepared plans for Chicago, San Francisco, New Haven, Boulder, Utica, and other cities. L'Enfant's original plan for Washington was revived and improved by the MacMillan Commission. It was truly an age of architectural art and urban pageantry.

For reasons of economy, the Tarnsey Act that financed City Beautiful was repealed in 1912. Outraged at the superficiality of the civic design approach, social reformers had gained the upper hand. Thus the City Beautiful was unofficially replaced by the City Efficient.

The period 1910-50 was one of extensive city planning undertaken by a distinguished company of enlightened and highly motivated professionals.

Early in the period planners were consultants—social and economic reformers, engineers, and architects. Their clients were local betterment, civic, and improvement associations. As the period advanced, "clients" tended to become official local planning boards and departments, and the planners became trained staff members.

In terms of the realization of plans, successes included a few new suburbs like Forest Hills and Sunnyside in New York and the four greenbelt towns that followed the direction of the selfmade British planner, Ebenezer Howard, whose remarkable 1902 publication called for limited population size, permanent greenbelts, balanced communities, and civic art.[4] Without the commerce and industry that would have made them real towns, these greenbelt towns—Radburn, New Jersey, Greenbelt, Maryland, Greenhills, Ohio, and Greendale, Wisconsin—actually became well-planned garden suburbs. Another success of the period was subdivision legislation that eventually convinced developers that money could be made in designing subdivisions attractively.

A third planning achievement was zoning in those cases in which legislation was actually written by professional planners (often it was written by lawyers) and to the extent that resultant legislation equitably served the public or helped to effect a desirable objective. Not an unequivocal achievement! One public segment has been particularly well served by zoning. The middle-income owner of a suburban house has been protected from industrial development next door and apartment development (poor people) across the street. Zoning is by its very nature a negative instrument and has had a restricted ability to realize urban improvement.

After years of struggle, the "housers" emerged victorious in 1937, largely responsible for the introduction of low-rent public housing through the U.S. Housing Act of that year. Led by Catherine Bauer, the vanguard housers included no city planners, per se, although planners provided support. The act actually snubbed city planners by not requiring local planning commission review before submission of a proposed project to the federal funding agency.

Bricks and mortar accomplishments were, however, the exception during the period; in these terms, 1910 marked the beginning of four decades of largely paper plans and fruitless city planning endeavors.

In the 1910s and 1920s it was the *master plan* that was expected to bring about improved cities. It did not turn out that way. City planner Thomas Adams observed in his 1935 book that out of the thousand or so plans prepared since 1910 "perhaps not more than one-fifth are being followed in some degree for guiding the development of cities."[5] At the conclusion of his book, Adams voiced what came to be the city planner's lament: "Too much planning has ended on paper and in pigeonholes."[6]

Next it was the *planning commission* that was going to make all the difference. Planning boards and commissions were thought to be capable of taking the politics out of urban development. A wish made in desperation, this expectation for planning commissions turned out to be an absurd fantasy. The reason is simple. By and large, people appointed by the city council to planning boards and commissions are unpaid responsible citizens, unschooled in planning techniques; they are accompanied by a few "ex officio" members, local staff officials. Without city council approval, a planning commission's rulings do not become law. The important point is this: elected city council members will not yield components of power to others unless the law demands it.

One of the earliest proponents of true legal power for planning commissions was John Quincy Adams (not the sixth president of the United States), who recommended to a Senate committee as far back as 1909 that every city government appoint a "permanent city planning commission" that would have complete control of all future development in the city.[7] Evidently the Senate was not ready to recommend such a sweeping transfer of power away from elected officials.

In the 1930s eminent planners reluctantly concluded that independent planning commissions were unable to carry out the planning function in American cities. Walter Blucher, executive director of the American Society of Planning Officials, maintained in 1937 that most of the 1,200 city planning commissions in America were moribund and served "no useful purpose." He found them to have "failed to function satisfactorily for many years" and to have "made no contribution to community development."[8] And Robert Averill Walker, author of a definitive 1941-50 planning text, found that the average planning commission member did not comprehend planning, was not particularly interested in its objectives and activities, and did not exercise a judgment superior to that of elected officials. In addition, he found a certain outrageousness in their very existence:

> In practice an executive and city council are asked to set up an agency which has the power to veto their actions and to embarrass the administration by criticizing its policies but which is responsible neither to them nor to the electorate. Their natural reluctance to subject themselves thus to review and criticism is supplemented by the prevalent sentiment among public officials that citizen boards are amateurish and of no great value.[9]

Then in the 1940s the favored means of achieving city planning was *the local planner slotted "right into the administration of local government,"* advising the mayor directly. Blucher was for it:

> I think that the main reason for the failure of planning lies in our neglect to consider planning as a part of the administration of gov-

ernment. We certainly have not sold administrators on the planning idea, and that largely because we haven't shown them that planning is essential to a good government. What the country needs is planning administrators or what I choose to call "planners," and I forecast that planning will never rise above its present status until such time as it is made an essential part of the governmental organization."[10]

Walker was just as emphatic:

It is high time that planning agencies were established firmly within the administrative hierarchy of municipal government. The heads of such agencies should be appointed by and be responsible to the chief executive. Along with this must go a long-time process of education for planners, administrators, and civic groups alike on their respective roles in governmental planning.[11]

Unfortunately, even though this solution sounds effective, there is no strength in it. The mayor has a planning staff, if he has one, probably because enlightened citizens demanded it somewhere along the line. The staff planner whose advice happens not to be desired by the mayor and city council has no legal recourse whatsoever. The city council still adopts all local laws, ordinances, and resolutions. If the mayor and the city council do not wish to be educated and enlightened by the planner, they have little difficulty ignoring his advice. If he goes public, he jeopardizes his entire career.

Walker's last sentence demonstrates a common failure of social reformers—the evocation of a curative entity that not enough people value. I am always intrigued by people who call for education to solve things, when the achievement of that goal requires a majority of already-educated people to insist on its embrace. Local administrators, especially those elected by the people, are usually unaware of their lack of education. They think they are as knowledgeable as anyone else. Often they think that education and planning are just fancy frills.

Metropolitan regional planning was vigorously promoted throughout the 1910-50 period and was established, at least for a time, in Chicago, Los Angeles, Philadelphia, and elsewhere. New York's flagship Regional Plan Association produced the *First Regional Plan* during the years 1929-65. Privately financed, its *Second Regional Plan* was brought out with great media fanfare in the 1960s and 1970s in a heroic effort to gain public support for its approach to regional growth and development. In a word, its principal approach was the clustering of commercial and cultural development in certain existing regional centers. The *Second Regional Plan's* weakest element was its woefully inadequate promotion of implementational measures. Unlike New York's effort, most metro-politician regional planning organizations have confined themselves to traffic and transportation, water supply and distribution, sewage, refuse, parks, flood control, and other relatively noncontroversial matters. All regional planning organizations have been advisory.

Metropolitan regional *government* has been advocated over and over again—in Boston, Minneapolis–St. Paul, and other cities—but it has been no match for established municipal home rule. Not surprisingly, opposition has come mainly from suburban communities. (By contrast, the Province of Ontario, Canada, in 1954 simply imposed a regional government on the Toronto metropolitan area for planning and public works development.)

The Housing Act of 1949 did not eliminate the weak planning devices and institutions of the previous four decades, but it strengthened city planning considerably. Under the act no urban renewal could be undertaken that was not based on a citywide plan approved by the governing body. Professional planners were hired to plan the city and renewal areas and help carry out the plans. The act gave the federal agency considerable authority in assuring that whatever was planned and approved was actually undertaken. This made it possible for local planners to stand up to wayward local politicians by evoking the authority of "the feds." ("The feds won't let us do that.") More important, the act provided substantial amounts of money to clear slums, entice desirable redevelopment, and renovate existing buildings.

One of the defects of the urban renewal progam as a mechanism for implementing significant urban improvement nationwide lay in the fact that only those cities that applied for funds got funds, and only those projects locally selected were federally considered. Thus many slum neighborhoods around the country remained severely blighted, while less blighted areas were cleared and redeveloped; the choice depended primarily on the caliber and the will of local elected officials. The act did not permit national planners to assure that federal money went where needs were greatest. (Such a provision would have been politically impossible at the time.) As local governments had to supply a fairly sizable percentage of renewal costs (between a third and a sixth), impoverished and unsophisticated cities were able to undertake fewer improvements than relatively healthy ones.

In addition, redevelopers tended to shy away from those slum districts not linked to marketable areas. Even inducements like almost-free cleared land did not succeed in offsetting the dangers of such investments in the minds of developers. Thus today, over forty years after renewal was first undertaken, devastating slum areas remain.

It is ironic that when urban renewal was replaced by President Nixon's "community development" program in 1974, formulas of city need were developed by the federal agency, with the money (supposedly) allocated to the cities accordingly. Local government's financial contribution became zero. The funds, however, were infinitesimal. The federal agency still did not stipulate worst neighborhoods first. Moreover, to broaden service to Republican localities, the number of recipient communities was expanded widely to include economically comfortable suburbs and downright rural places containing tiny pockets of "poverty." The small pot of money was spread too thin. By the middle 1980s the extent of federal oversight became laughable. How to spend community development funds has been left more and more to local determination. Only 20 percent was supposed to go to administration, with 15 percent for social services, but with tepid, after-the-fact oversight, development funds could be squandered on administrative salaries rather than actual projects in the very cities that needed renewal most. Thus the community development program has been no real mechanism for the advancement of city planning or the resolution of renewal needs.

A few successful new towns were built in the 1960s, notably Reston, Virginia, and Columbia, Maryland. Two were built by New York State's Urban Development Corporation in the early 1970s: Audubon near Buffalo and Radisson near Syracuse. All told the list of post–World War II new towns comes to nine or ten nationwide.

Although urban renewal was the most effective of post–1950 city planning instruments, at best its scope was limited as well. It was powerless against those other major forces shaping America in the twentieth century: the tremendous private car explosion, the decay of mass transit, the relentless horrors of urban schools, the outflux of the middle-income group, the influx of poor, growing ghettoization, the continuous spread of outlying shopping centers, overdevelopment in metropolitan centers, land speculation, municipal corruption, and entrepreneurial greed.

Throughout its existence the city planning profession has not trained or encouraged local planners to first examine a city's economic and physical needs in a thorough manner, and then follow this up with recommendations and priorities for meeting those needs—in essence true planning. On the contrary, the jurisdiction of a planner has been constrained. Each piece of the planning profession's allotment has been tacked on at some point over the years, either as a municipal expediency, or, more often, as a reaction to a horror of the day. Thus the assortment spreads out as follows:

**City Planning's Assortment of Professional Concerns
with Years of Introduction**

1870-90

    Housing

    Public Utilities (sanitation, sewerage)

1890-1910

> Parks and recreation
>
> Public buildings
>
> City appearance (urban design)

1910-50

> Population
>
> Land use
>
> Economic base
>
> Transportation
>
> New towns (suburbs)
>
> Zoning
>
> Subdivisions
>
> Official map
>
> Capital improvement programming
>
> Master planning (comprehensive planning)

1950-92

> Urban renewal
>
>> Slum clearance
>>
>> Redevelopment
>>
>> Rehabilitation
>>
>> Citizen participation
>
> Historic preservation
>
> Industrial development
>
> Environmental impacts

Major urban concerns are left out of this assortment. The most blatant omission is *the urban school.* Although the urban school represents a vital component of the urban community, city planners are not supposed to touch. The Board of Education undertakes all planning exclusively. Local planners are so accustomed to this exclusion, they accept whatever the Board of Education specifies. Not only has the substandard urban school played a lethal role in the continuous outflux of the middle-income group, the urban school is also significant to planners as the conceptual focus of neighborhoods and a magnet for family involvement in community life (concepts sometimes necessarily and unfortunately thwarted by busing of schoolchildren to counteract defacto segregation). To validate my point: The International City Managers' Association (ICMA) books, *Local Planning Administration* (1941-59) and *Principles and Practice of Urban Planning* (1968), the official city planning textbooks, have no chapter on schools. The subject is omitted entirely from the former text; in the 1968 volume schools are mentioned only briefly under another topic.[12]

Many other elements of urban life are hands off to planners, and traditional planners do not like to confuse things by studying broad community topics—for example, the human settlement alternatives of Israeli *kibbutzim* (collective farms). When I included the subject of the kibbutz in a lecture at Pratt, I was told by a fellow instructor that kibbutzim had nothing to do with planning. He meant "planning." He meant the subject was not included in the assortment.

Tending to the *official map* and preparing the *capital improvement program* became parts of the city planner's assortment for reasons of conspiratorial expediency, I suspect. Official mapping is a technical activity that was undoubtedly undertaken by engineers and lawyers before city planning came along. It has absolutely nothing to do with planning once the street system has been established or planned. It is planning the way carpentry is architecture. One might assume, however, that capital improvement programming, which was formerly undertaken by a municipal budget director, sensibly belongs in the planner's bailiwick. The capital improvement program covers five or six years and is kept updated; the first year supposedly constitutes the next capital budget. It may not. In terms of results, capital programming is frequently a useless exercise: the planning director undertakes a great deal of work that comes to naught because in the end, the annual capital budget the city council actually passes is entirely different, prepared probably by the budget director a week before deadline. Why use the term "conspiratorial"? One answer is that a planning director tied up with official mapping and capital improvement programming cannot get into too many urbanistic causes and reforms.

I know of no better example of the typical American planning record than Karl Belser's account of what happened to Santa Clara County, California, after World War II. Belser was county planning director from 1950 to 1967, and his story, published in the Fall 1970 issue of *Cry California*, demonstrates to me that West Coast land under development pressures has experienced the same kind of greedy, chaotic development so well known to the eastern megalopolis. His agonizing story proves once again that even the most vigilant American planning director has been powerless against these forces.

In the nineteenth century the Santa Clara Valley grew to become a lush agricultural paradise, primarily because of its remarkable topsoil of fine loam (30 to 40 feet in places), its artesian water, and a subtropical climate. Products were prunes, fruit trees, and the voluminous quantities of grapes essential for an extensive wine industry. Between 1870 and 1940 an ideal agricultural system developed in the valley. Together with agriculture-oriented industries located in the cities and towns of San Jose (the county seat), Alviso, Palo Alto, Mountain View, Sunnyvale, Santa Clara, and Los Gatos, the Santa Clara Valley became a perfectly integrated agricultural community. Wineries, canneries, financial and professional services, distributors to world markets—all components of the agricultural industry were located within the valley itself. Thus for seventy years the valley was a beautiful and wholesome place in which to live and work, and the county was rated one of the fifteen most productive agricultural counties in the nation.

World War II marked the beginning of the end of this ideal community. During the war Stanford University near Palo Alto specialized in the development of sophisticated electronic military equipment, a fact that was to have a marked impact on postwar development. In addition, thousands of servicemen traveled through this magnificent and peaceful valley on their way to the war's Pacific theater or were brought to the valley for training and processing. These young men and women formed the first wave of a huge postwar market for housing there. Indeed, between 1950 and 1955 the valley became inundated with new development.

Meanwhile in 1950 the people of San Jose elected an aggressive administration that had massive goals for expansion and growth without qualifications or restraints. Belser points out that a carefully worked out policy for change and growth by the community's power structure "might have allowed the cities to grow more slowly and to incorporate and control urban expansion, while the rural areas could have remained as essential base to much of the older structure."[13]

But contemplation of such an alternative was far from what actually happened. Instead, speculators took over and in effect pushed the county into uncontrolled development. The behavior of all elements of the community during the time from 1950 to 1965 can best be described as pandemonium. Wild urban growth attacked the valley much as cancer attacks the human body. People poured into the area in vast numbers. The land began to be covered with houses, streets, schools, freeways, factories and all the related services required by this new population. Huge sums were made available to build freeways and expressways which made the urban explosion possible. Landowners sold out under the pressure of rising taxes and the great opportunity to make large gains on the value of the land. Misled by the fiction that growth and development would lead to economic solvency, government sold out to business and industry by making many concessions inimical to the public interest as inducements for development investment, while the power structure, led by the financial institutions, the media, the wealthy urban property owners and the business community, exploited the situation to make huge profits. In less than 20 years the valley became the home and place of work for more than a million people. What so recently had been a beautiful productive garden was suddenly transformed into an urban anthill.

Not only was the new development an encroachment on the prime agricultural land, but the result was an uneconomical, wasteful and fiscally insolvent mess. The scattered nature of the development and its uneven quality produced a pattern requiring the provision of urban services of all kinds on a most uneconomical basis. The public costs of these services have produced a per-capita debt which is among the highest in the state of California. The social dislocation was equally critical, with a large portion of the farm-oriented labor force, unable to adjust to the new pace, ultimately finding its way to the welfare rolls while people with more sophisticated skills came into the valley to take the jobs offered by the new scientifically oriented industries. Simultaneously, serious physical problems began to emerge, such as increased flooding which resulted from covering the absorbent soil with buildings and asphalt, and the subsidence of the land caused by the lowering of the water table to serve new urban demands. These, together with traffic congestion and air and water pollution, continue to this day to require costly remedial action.[14]

Without a plan for growth endorsed by the elected officials, small farmers had to make their own choices between hanging on or selling out and taking a huge gain on the land price. The least successful farmers sold out, and these inflated sales prompted the assessor to increase the tax value of remaining agricultural land, basing this course of action on the steep prices of recent sales. For the remaining farmers this of course created a financial crisis. Even more damaging was the enormous increase in the tax rate brought about by the explosion of new schools, sewers, fire protection, and other urban services.

Until the mid-1950s, the remaining farmers held to their century-old suspicion of governmental intervention. When in 1954-55 they tried to achieve various kinds of legislation to limit urbanization, the cities wildly annexed any and all available unincorporated land. (Cities can do this in some parts of the country, for example, the West and Southwest.) City jurisdictions assumed chaotic configurations. San Jose, for example, became a hideous amalgam of scattered and dispersed land developments, wasted land resources, and ridiculous boundary patterns. From the air San Jose gave the appearance of a jigsaw puzzle with half the pieces missing. A Stanford Environmental Law Society study of its land use tells why:

Several explicit policies pursued by the city government virtually

guaranteed that San Jose would assume its present state. These policies assured that development would take place not necessarily
where the inhabitants as a whole wanted it nor where reason dictated, but where the developers chose to build. And developers most
often chose to build where land could be obtained at the least
expense, usually in undeveloped areas substantially beyond the
inhabited perimeter of the city.

Without government encouragement, or at least accommodation,
these developers would have found it unprofitable to locate in such
disperse locations. Speculation was made profitable only through
city cooperation in annexation, extension of necessary sewers, storm
drains, and roads.[15]

Seven unincorporated communities, frightened by the orgy of annexa-
tions, formed themselves into incorporated cities in the 1950s, bringing
the total of county municipalities to sixteen. The county and each of the
towns and cities enacted their own development codes. Thus development
became "regulated" by seventeen zoning ordinances, building codes, and
standards for community building. Not surprisingly, architects and
builders became confused and thwarted by the multitude of differing
laws, while speculators took advantage of the zoning jumble and avoided
observing controls wherever possible.

Although building codes were designed to be *minimum* standards,
"merchant builders" used them as if they were specifications for design.
This brought about the minimum-standard house, which of course
became substandard within a very short period—the "instant slum."

All of this was done with the aid of the FHA. It was not the homeowner, in whose interest the agency was originally founded, who
came to the FHA office with a proposal, but a tract developer who
wished to take advantage of the attractive interest rate, the insured
mortgage, the built-in opportunity for a no-risk profit. He wished to
build hundreds of look-alike homes in rows of 50- by 100-foot lots to
be sold to a market in desperate need and with very little choice.

The developers used every means at their disposal to beat down
any resistance to their plans in the regional office of the FHA and to
bully the local agencies in charge of controlling development. Thus
septic tank sewage-disposal systems were approved in tract development. At one time there were roughly 30,000 such installations
serving urban subdivisions in the county. Many of them were poorly
installed and were a source of serious health problems which had to
be corrected later at the owners' expense. This kind of laxity gave a
free hand to the creators of urban sprawl and made local control
very difficult.

The Veterans Administration was even more lax than the FHA, and such marginal developments as those constructed by Brandon Enterprises (Lakewood Village and Tropicana Village) were underwritten by the VA and allowed to be built in what were historically known to be floodplains. Not only were the houses built with minimum standards all the way around, it was a certainty that they would be flooded. They were, and at one time there were over 400 units in the county that were abandoned by their purchasers, all of which reverted to the government for rehabilitation and resale. The protection which had to be provided became the responsibility of the city taxpayer.[16]

By 1970 the valley's 300-square-mile area was almost entirely developed, primarily with subdivisions and large industries, subsequently dubbed "Silicon Valley." Belser's aerial photographs of 1950 and 1970 vividly illustrate what twenty years of chaotic development had wrought. Not only is the loss of this prime farmland a tragedy, the rapacious development he described should not have occurred—anywhere. As indicated, the problems that emanated from it included a monstrous debt, water supply problems, air pollution, noise pollution, land subsidence, flooding, and incredible traffic congestion—traffic congestion not solvable by mass transit because of the random development patterns.

While the responsibility for what happened to the Santa Clara Valley (and to almost every growing urban community across the nation) is laid at the door of local governments and special interests, surely both the state of California and the federal government must share some of the blame. Federal programs—housing, highways, defense contracts, etc.—speeded, not hindered, the destruction. And the state, lacking and never seeking any clear notion of how the lands of California should be utilized, stood by idly, apparently powerless to check the onslaught.[17]

To those interested in further details of the "flagrant ruination of the Santa Clara Valley," I commend the entire article, probably available in large libraries.[18] The article elaborates on the myriad problems caused by greedy entrepreneurs, local governments that equate developmental growth with prosperity and therefore eagerly welcome any kind of new development, apathetic state and federal agencies, and a frail system of urban planning.

This story provides a perfect paradigm of my central thesis that, generally speaking, urban planning has no effect on urban development in this country because urban planning has not been legally organized to make a difference. Despite repeated advice and protestations to the governing officials over a seventeen-year period, Karl Belser was unable as county planner to prevent the chaotic development that occurred.

NOTES

1. Reps, *The Making of Urban America*, and Tunnard and Reed, *American Skyline*.

2. Reps, *The Making of Urban America*, p. 474.

3. Lewis Mumford, *The Story of Utopias* (New York: Boni & Liveright, 1922).

4. Ebenezer Howard, *Garden Cities of Tomorrow* (London: Faber & Faber, Ltd., 1902).

5. Thomas Adams, *Outline of Town and City Planning* (New York: Russell Sage Foundation), 1935, p. 213.

6. Ibid., p. 327.

7. Ibid., p. 210.

8. Walter Blucher quoted in Mel Scott, *American City Planning Since 1890* (Berkeley: University of California Press, 1969), pp. 330-31.

9. Robert Averill Walker, *The Planning Function in Urban Government* (Chicago: University of Chicago Press, 1941 and 1950), p. 164.

10. Walter H. Blucher in a letter quoted in ibid., p. 179.

11. Walker, *The Planning Function*, p. 370.

12. Finally, in its 1979 version, *Practice of Local Government Planning*, ICMA includes a chapter entitled "Educational Services."

13. Karl Belser, "The Making of Slurban America," *Cry California* (Fall 1970), p. 5.

14. Ibid., pp. 5-6.

15. Stanford Environmental Law Society, "San Jose's Self-Destruct Policies," *Cry California* (Fall 1970), p. 9. (This short article from the *San Jose Land Use Study* is an inset within Belser's article.)

16. Belser, "The Making of Slurban America," pp. 15, 17.

17. Ibid., p. 18.

18. Ibid., p. 1.

4

Local Planning

LOCAL PLANNING ACTIVITIES

"What's it like being a planner?" I have been asked. "What does a planner do?" For a start, a new planning director gets to know the city inside and out. The procedure involves reading all the published material available, as well as viewing every block of the area personally. This is followed by numerous discussions with relevant local officials and civic leaders for both information and advice. After a few months of research, the planner may prepare, as a point of departure, an initial "thrust report" consisting of what he finds to be the city's banes and benefits, as well as the planning principles, short-term goals, long-term goals, operational principles, special studies and programs, and means of implementation he intends to pursue. Banes can be such problems as low tax rate, insufficient housing for a particular income group, trucking through the downtown, erstwhile corrupt government, inadequate public transit, and the like. Benefits can include such factors as progressive new local administration, increasingly supportive citizenry, abundant private dollars, ample relocation resource housing, and the like. In addition the planner tries to identify any potential development projects that might be capable of spearheading improvement of the entire city.

The local planner may initially prepare prototype studies in which quantities are assumed for illustrative purposes—for instance the number of garden apartments, potential rents, local revenues expected—in order to demonstrate the fiscal feasiblity of her more radical ideas.

Depending on the quality and timeliness of existing plans and ordinances, the new planner will prepare or update a master plan, zoning ordinance, community renewal program, subdivision ordinance, capital improvement program, and/or undertake other continuing responsibilities.

The type of local government involved dictates whether this material is prepared initially for the planning board, for the development administrator, or for the mayor or city manager. If a proposal is to be presented to the city council, it is presented, in most cities, through the planning board or chief executive, rather than independently by the local planner. The planning staff prepares material and resolutions for consideration by the planning board and city council, and possibly the historic preservation commission and the board of zoning appeals. In some cities the local planner may be involved in building permit review and design review. He attends meetings with numerous leaders—the mayor, heads of other city departments, the city council, the planning board, the historic preservation commission, the environmental commission, neighborhood groups, civic and religious leaders, and standing or ad hoc committees. These activities may well involve one or two evening meetings a week.

In any given week, the local planner's continuing work may well be interrupted by a proposal that has been unexpectedly presented to the mayor by a potential private developer or civic group for a particular site. The mayor may well ask the planning director to review this proposal and provide a recommendation. (When a development proposal conforms to the zoning and other local laws, and when the developer wants no special assistance from the city, this kind of review and approval is not required.) Research, mapping, calculations, and discussions are of course required for the planning department's review. In the event that the local planner is opposed to the proposal as presented, and if she has convinced the mayor as to the wisdom of her position, her staff may prepare an alternative plan for the site, supported by specific research, explicit rationale, and persuasive pro formas. The civic group or developer in question may return with still a third version, starting the process all over again. This kind of jockeying and bargaining may go on for weeks before a final decision is reached by the mayor and city council. Thus while the local planner initiates much of her own work, a good portion may be reactive to outside proposals.

QUASI-EFFECTIVE STRATEGIES

An essential local planning procedure, one that stands the planner in good stead throughout his career, is that of considering carefully, before deciding on a planning course of action, all its procedures and steps, and its potential benefits and defects—in other words, anticipating all the unintended consequences potentially to result from the course of action. (Somewhat tongue in cheek is the concomitant "principle" that if something beneficial unexpectedly results from a plan, the planner is expected to imply that these benefits were anticipated all along.)[1]

A dedicated planning director can work with integrity within city government by fighting fiercely for her views within, and only within, the administration. However, once a decision is made on an issue by the mayor or city council, the planner accepts the decision, even if she is overruled. She accepts defeat and gets on to the next issue. (Acceptance does not include speaking and writing in favor of an issue she has professionally opposed.)

Typically, a local planner is no star, no charismatic leader. Very often he is part of a hardworking team that has been advised by the mayor not to talk to the media. The real brains in planning are not writers or critics but day-to-day professionals who keep their mouths shut publicly in order to pursue their work. Moreover, they are not looking for quick and easy answers, for they appreciate that their work is complex in the extreme. Although most urban problems would not be too difficult to sort out if they could be approached separately, in urban affairs everything you touch disturbs thirty other things.

In hiring her staff the action-oriented planner selects idealistic, pragmatic, action-oriented reformers like herself, conducts careful and thorough research to support her hypotheses, and develops conservative pro formas to prove they will work. Plans are presented and illustrated with gusto. And the team never gives up, not until the outcome is clear.

Planning staff attends en masse any meetings with other city departments on important planning issues. This strategy is employed because the local planner needs voices. There might be ten to fifteen other staff members in the room, hailing from entirely different disciplines, each harboring the firmly held opinion that planning solutions are all common sense, each eager to voice some half-baked, unsubstantiated idea to which the mayor might well give equal attention. If you are only one planner in a meeting like this, you have only one voice against all these contributors. Thus an unwritten "rule of meetings" maintains that when your views are in the minority, your effectiveness in making policy is directly proportional to the number of voices espousing your message. A pleasant but persistent planning voice can climb right into the discussion as another planner's voice is starting to trail off or as the planning group is in danger of being swamped by the interlopers. A dedicated planner cannot succeed if his ego misdirects him to try to do all the persuading alone. In local government one man's pearls of wisdom are another man's stuff and nonsense.

MASTER PLANNING

Master planning, as we have seen, has been a major function of the profession since 1910, and it is axiomatic that an overall plan is pivotal to the orderly improvement of urban areas. The usual master plan (also called a comprehensive or general plan) is a spiral-bound document providing relevant data on existing conditions, much from the U.S. Census, and goals for the future in terms of land use, circulation, local economy, downtown development, neighborhood improvement, and the like. These elements are presented visually, statistically, and in narrative form. Some master plans are detailed and consist of several volumes, others are brief. Except in states like New Jersey, which encourages the inclusion of specific elements, master plans vary considerably. It is not uncommon for a master plan to include very few proposals for change, consisting almost entirely of compilations of existing conditions. Moreover, master plan language tends to be euphemistic and bland, sometimes giving a tone of acceptability to existing conditions that are in truth alarming. (This may be vividly seen in Chapter 6.) In this connection, master plans could be greatly improved through the use of physical and social deficiencies surveys of neighborhoods, using real terms, such as: "derelict cars on streets and lots," "exposed garbage on sidewalks," "trash-strewn public areas," based on visual surveys, or "extent of child prostitution," "extent of joblessness," based on social research.

Another appalling commonplace in master planning is that of preparing an entire plan without benefit of even one field trip, using printed documents as the sole source of information. This has been done in major cities, as well as small ones. Although documents yield much needed information, probably more than any other source, an area cannot be properly planned that has not been seen by the planners.

When federal funding for city renewal was more plentiful than it is today, action-oriented planners questioned the validity and usefulness of master plans as they were typically prepared and used. Too often a master plan was written solely for the purpose of applying for federal funds under certain programs. As these programs usually fell far short of meeting the city's total needs, within the plan the needs of the community were shrunk, consciously or unconsciously, to fit the programs. What the master plan usually consisted of was an inadequate and incomplete description of existing conditions and a set of recommendations geared to dollars conceivably available from various funding sources. No attempt was made to spell out the extent to which the master plan's remedies would assuredly make everything right. Whatever funding was available at the time was suggested as the appropriate solution. This describes today's master plans as well, except that today only a comparative trickle of federal (or state) money is funneled to the cities.

People exposed to master plans tend to wonder at some point who on earth is reading these plans. To my knowledge, the master plan is *meant* to be read primarily by (1) decision-makers: the mayor, city council, city planning commission, zoning commission, building commissioner, and the like (frequently they do not), and (2) interested local citizens (more often they do). A copy is usually sent to the local library. But although there may be a mailing to known citizens groups, there is no comprehensive mailing to residents. Normally, interested persons can get a copy as long as copies last. Distribution is therefore catch as catch can.

By and large, master plans are neither adopted by the planning commission/city council nor complied with. If a significant site is developed according to the master plan, this constitutes a concidence, in most cases. An eastern city with which I was once familiar had a different master plan prepared every three to five years and totally ignored all of them. Every one of these plans was "just gathering dust," I was told—a city planning cliché.

Things have improved somewhat in New Jersey towns. The master plan is used as a firm basis for zoning in that state; its land use and housing elements must be complied with in zoning unless the municipality's governing body takes certain fairly stringent and conspicuous steps to so avoid. Since the mid-1980s the trend in New Jersey's municipalities has been toward more, rather than less, planning. Master plans (and thus to a large extent zoning ordinances) normally include all the elements outlined in the state's *Municipal Land Use Law*, and the courts have recently given further support to zoning ordinances that control such concerns as open-space preservation, location of municipal facilities, and the like. All 567 New Jersey municipalities have zoning; most have adopted master plans. Unfortunately, the exceptions to this consistency are the larger cities, the problems of which are onerous and seemingly insurmountable.

A rather radical approach to master planning would be to tell all—to set down all a city's needs in a first section, including priorities, plans for correction and costs, followed by a second section that addresses currently available means of implementation and funds available. In the event that funding programs fell considerably short of satisfying the need, as they have historically, this deficit would be made clear in this section of the master plan. Interested citizens would then be able to petition their political representatives and nonprofit organizations in an effort to put funding in line with needs. To my knowledge this has never been done.

Local elected officials might well find public exposure to such a deficit program detrimental to various of their own objectives, including, very possibly, that of keeping the middle class within the city. But the very problems thus described would, if left unchecked, ineluctably lead to increased crime and other evils, ultimately pushing the middle class out of the city, anyway. The rub is that local elected officials usually do not concern themselves with problems that may develop "ultimately." They run for election every two to four years and address short-term problems as much as possible. Citizen knowledge of these urban dangers is therefore necessary to bring about change. Thus with a tell-all master plan that is well distributed, concerned residents could face up to the total package of problems and demand the means of correcting them before they multiplied, for we know they will multiply (have multiplied) until they cannot effectively be hidden away in another section of town, until they finally permeate the entire city.

PRINCIPLES

City planning can be and often is perfunctory, elementary, inauthentic, and irrelevant, whether it is implementable or not, and this brings us to the question of what sound planning consists of. In addition to those previously expressed, some elements of good planning, in my opinion, are briefly described as follows. (Those that specifically deal with urban redevelopment are discussed in Chapter 7.)

Planning for an urban area of any size requires a major framework of basic planning components and patterns that form the infrastructure out of which smaller-scale improvements can be developed, including renewal projects, public facility construction, commercial and industrial development, and the like. The framework plan must bring solid economic advances for the city in the very near future, as well as the more distant future. Something dramatic is also needed as a spur, to provide inspiration, and good plans will attempt to balance these two, supported by thorough and reliable technical and economic investigation. Putting things in balance is a major part of good planning. "Something dramatic" sets a major goal in motion, as one element of urban life builds upon another, producing a chain reaction of private interests that will carry it along.

In following the mutual benefits principle, discussed in Chapter 1, the planner addresses improvements skillfully and sensitively, with the result that even opposing forces realize major benefits. Every proposed change sets up a challenge in this connection, and the excitement to a good planner is in trying to meet it.

Advance planning should be done continuously to anticipate trends and problems, and to avoid crisis-to-crisis reactions. Work done merely in response to sudden demand, without enlightened hypotheses and research in place, turns out to be both difficult and invalid. In some cases this means developing an information bank of vital statistics and facts about the city, as well as contacting other cities for their experience and solutions to common problems. In other cases it means getting into design studies to point entrepreneurs in the direction the city wants development to go. If that does not work, a good way to bring developers or mayors around to good planning or design is to use their own objectives, wherever possible, rather than attempting to convince them that a certain planning or design rationale is valid or important. In the case of developers these objectives usually concern development costs, while those of mayors and city managers typically come down to jobs and revenues. Surprisingly, perhaps, good planning or urban design often turns out to be the most economically effective of several alternatives.

Working in local government provides a probing, committed planner countless opportunities to test and reevaluate professional principles. Planners have been accused of engendering projects that are impractical simply because their concepts are new to the city in question. Pedestrian malls in old downtowns represent a good example. Initially shopkeepers are terrified of them—largely because of their newness—when logic should tell them that customers walk into shops on two feet, not on four tires. Critical requirements are: *adjacent* parking, convenient loading and unloading, and smooth-running traffic and transportation lanes paralleling the mall. If these fundamental needs are satisfied, sales in pedestrian malls tend to skyrocket.

Equally axiomatic is the principle that everything indispensable to a plan must be included and workable, much like the parts of an automobile engine, if it is to be called a true plan. No vital component can be left out, no matter how numerous these essential parts. A workable solution is certainly not the same as an initially-acceptable solution, and a good planner can establish the workability of a plan, using comparable facts to demonstrate feasibility, even if all the naysayers find it unacceptable initially.

An essential component to any plan is the market. No plan has a chance of succeeding unless there are more than enough potentially interested people capable of supporting it, by virtue of income, geographic distance, and desire. It is as simple as that. This is as true for a bus route as it is for a grocery store, as true for a downtown shopping complex as it is for a waterfront residential community. A project's market does not have to be proven in advance, however. Experience, imagination, and judgment are as important as facts in determining a potential market in the case of an exciting new concept.

Promotional presentations of major developmental ideas and approaches, using attractive visual aids, can serve several important functions: provide valuable information to decision-makers, give confidence and inspiration to the planning team, and perhaps most important, cumulatively combine to represent a strong promotional force, more capable of competing with disinterested or opposing forces than fragmented discussions or written statements.

These are just a few of the principles and practices that make up sound planning. What planning tends to be like under the stringent limitations of state and local law and political philosophy are the subjects of Chapters 5 and 6.

NOTE

1. See also Martin Meyerson and Edward C. Banfield, *Politics, Planning, and the Public Interest* (New York: The Free Press of Glencoe, 1955), pp. 313-21.

5

Myths about City Planning

The myths discussed here are implied, rather than expressed, and have come to my attention as I have practiced and observed city planning over a forty-year period. They are: the planner as doctor myth, the myth of the planner as a member of the local political team, the mayor and city council as enlightened statesmen myth, and the myth that effective local planning can easily occur in American cities.

THE PLANNER AS DOCTOR MYTH

The city planner is *not* to a troubled city what a physician is to a human patient, although civic leaders who support a planning department sometimes have this initial impression. The word "doctor" is used here as the professional person who has answers, who knows the latest and best solutions, and takes action.

The work of the city planning profession is extremely difficult owing to its complexity, lack of true political or legal support, and locally-insoluble problems. The tremendous obstacles encountered in attempting to take action make moments of personal gratification, after weeks and months of hard work, extremely rare. This relative absence of personal gratification has tended to keep out of the profession many intelligent, dedicated, and motivated people, leaving the field wide open to unpersuaded people looking for well-paid, fairly easy employment. Thus the field has become invaded by posturing shirkers who eventually move up into top positions and effect no real ends.

This trend was greatly assisted by a virtual open-door admissions policy at most graduate schools in the 1950s and 1960s in response to the clarion call for urban planners in those years. These deliberately lax entrance standards ultimately brought great detriment to the planning profession by the resultant abnormally small proportion of committed, confident professionals. This in turn meant that the needs of the cities frequently had an almost mute spokesman in the city planner.

Since World War II too many planners have tended to be profession-oriented and means-oriented. If the profession is in any way analogous to medicine, then the patient lies critically ill while the physicians ignore her and engross themselves in discussions of AMA criteria and prospective instruments for diagnosis. The task at hand is virtually bypassed. The magnitude of the problem may well have produced a lesser rather than a greater dedication to solution and action.

The Ph.D. in planning, introduced in the 1950s, eventually resulted in academic planners out of touch with what it meant to practice planning at the local level. In an extremely complex field, practical experience is essential for understanding, for communication, and certainly for leadership. Training in American city planning is unstandardized. A student can usually avoid difficult but vital subjects like development financing even if they are offered. In addition, an employee who is not educated in planning at all may be given a planning title if he or she has started at the bottom and learned planning on the job. These educational characteristics are indeed miles away from medicine.

City planning cannot be said to be respected by the public generally, a large proportion of whom—perhaps a majority—have never heard of it.

The city planner is not considered a doctor by the local political leadership, certainly. Any respect she may receive there is fragile and fleeting. And, as we have seen, other members of the local bureaucracy—the departments of engineering, public works, and building, for example—typically think city planning is common sense masquerading as an arcane discipline. You will not find this group treating our local planner as a doctor nor her master plan as a prescription.

What about developers? By and large, a potential developer does not ask to see a city's planner or master plan when he drives into town with a major proposal. He asks to see the mayor. The mayor does not call in the planning director at that point. Nor does he refer to the master plan. He has forgotten all about it, if he ever saw it. The planner may be asked at some point down the line if he "can live with the developer's proposal"—not asked whether or not the latter is in accord with the city's plan. This is not a cynical overstatement. This is the way it is, over and over again, nationwide.

Allan B. Jacobs, former planning director of San Francisco, points out in connection with a particularly disturbing defeat having to do with a major development project:

> Some developers and architects concluded, correctly, that they could bypass the process established by the planning staff to develop urban design guidelines for particularly sensitive projects. Instead, developers could go to the mayor, or to some of the commissioners, or perhaps to the chief administrative officer and get early backing. While there is nothing new about this practice, it invariably leaves the city planning staff on the losing side, and it had not been common for two years in San Francisco. The informal but effective design review process had been weakened considerably.[1]

A totally false assumption persists, furthermore, that local elected officials will actually read a city's master plan, after which they will make intelligent choices based on it. In practice, however, the mayor, city council, and other elected officials tend to shun the master plan, have in fact an aversion to even thumbing through it. A city's master plan is typically kept on a shelf at city hall gathering the proverbial dust—a prevalent result, as we have seen, bitterly deplored by Thomas Adams as long ago as 1935[2] (see Chapter 3). Corroborating this point is the Stanford (California) Environmental Law Society's *San Jose Land Use Study* of 1970, which found that the only body that appeared to respect San Jose's general (master) plan was the San Jose planning department itself. Moreover, local zoning officials and others were extremely suspicious of planning scholarship in general. In the society's own words:

> The real cause of zoning impotence lies in the administration which applies it. From the people to whom we have talked and from our own observations, it seems clear that the majority of the decisions on zoning are made on the basis of other considerations than the General Plan. The one city body which seems to take the General Plan seriously in their deliberations is the Planning Department. Their recommendations to the Planning Commission on rezonings, prezonings, variances and the like are based largely on the General Plan. The Planning Department itself, and as far as we can tell, the Planning Commission, sees this as being its proper role.
> The ironic result, however, is that the influence of the Planning Department is probably hurt by this. Whatever it says tends to be dismissed as just a "book" result by the Commissioners, an attitude which supplements their own intention to "humanize" the zoning process and helps justify their treatment of the General Plan. . . . Beyond the Planning Department . . . the General Plan gets little real credence in decision making. . . . While this would be difficult

to substantiate, we feel that we can demonstrate that rezonings are regularly granted which are not in accord with the General Plan.[3]

In my own experience, a city councilman, a relatively pleasant and responsible person, publicly likened the master plan we had recently produced to "all other master plans" for the city, even though its proposals took a completely different direction. He had neither read it nor attended the presentation describing it.

Local political leaders invariably trust the word of an outside economic consultant over that of their own planning staff. Indeed, the opinion of the outsider seems to be sacred to local leaders who are eager to pay many thousands of dollars, sometimes in six figures, to be given recommendations identical to those that have been proffered by their local planner in recent months. Moreover, the consultant's report commonly borrows heavily from analysis and data previously prepared by the local planner's office.

While the typical developer rides into town in the style of a four-star general, the dedicated local planner is in the infantry, fortified by a tiny body of law to support his place in land-policy decision-making, getting very little help from academic, private-agency, state, or federal planners. His personal risk is extremely high. As planning director, he is out there alone, often having to stand up to the "practical" local officials who, as we have seen, see no need for planning in the first place, everything being completely obvious, who oppose change, and who want the economic market to make as many decisions as possible. These officials may also expect a bribe here and there from importunate developers, a connection with which the planner might inadvertently interfere.

And to make her professional life more burdensome, the dedicated planner has to be her own fife and drum corps. In addition to devoting her energies to the potential development and implementation of solutions to urban problems, she is obliged unceasingly to convince people that she should be listened to, that planning is important. With a real property legal system that normally does not include "approval by the planning director" as a requirement, she has no choice. Unlike physicians and other professionals, the committed planner is forced to proselytize on a regular basis about the significance of her work and the value of her services.

THE MYTH OF THE PLANNER AS A MEMBER OF THE LOCAL POLITICAL TEAM

The committed local planner must constantly maneuver and promote himself within the administration in order to remain involved in developmental activities, but he must continually guard against the reality that any friendliness growing between him and those in power may soften his resolve and threaten his integrity.

The dedicated planner who is a member of the local political team is a great rarity. Where it exists, such membership is usually short-lived. He is trained to give his honest views, based on straight-forward research. His principal client is the city, while the mayor's principal focus is his political career. Eventually these two motivations clash. If the planner is pulled into opportunism at this point, he is no longer a dedicated planner. If he holds his ground, he is dropped off the political team and cut out of all negotiations with developers, although he may be retained as local planner, functioning in the usual independent or isolated manner.

In old cities with many problems, the mayor and council frequently have no commitment to do the job necessary and are interested primarily in furthering their careers. The poorer the city, the less the commitment. Such officials keep hidden agendas, giving lip service to important issues raised.

In such cities, despite strong, well-documented planning advice, the mayor's decisions can be dictated by a behind-the-scenes political party leader whose true agenda may not include solutions that benefit the city, but benefit instead the state, the county, or himself.

A mayor may not want to discuss a rational, well-worked-out analysis of an issue, for ulterior reasons. It is not uncommon, in fact, for such an official to request that the planner prepare an "objective analysis" of an issue only after a political decision has been made.

Political favoritism can be rife in local government, where council members make every effort to have their cronies hired, as opposed to qualified professionals. In this connection, finding work in one's own community is virtually impossible for a committed planner—either the community is too small to have a planner on the staff or it is so large that virtually all the staff appointments are chosen along political party lines. If the planner finds a responsible job within commuting distance, she may find herself unseated down the road when a planner residing in the community starts working for the political party in power and sets sights on her job.

Incidentally, a reform mayor can get into a similar predicament with his own party. After terminating the practice of bribery in the building department, say, or eliminating the city's practice of hiring untrained relatives of party regulars as schoolteachers, such a reform mayor may be under intense pressure to return "to normal" as soon as possible. If he consistently refuses, the party—his own party—may go so far as to refuse to back him for reelection. Particularly in cities that need a lot of help, reform is not popular with the local rulers, good ideas are not popular with the party behind the rulers, and straight thinking to help the people and the city carries little weight.

A classic case with which I am acquainted helps to refute the myth in question. Geographically the affected city was generally a long rectangle, its struggling downtown located at the center. Out of the blue, one day, a big-city shopping mall developer entered the scene, proposing to build a regional shopping mall on a large vacant site at one extremity of the city, about three miles from downtown. Such a proposal was, of course, a horrendous violation of all that is sensible in city planning. First, an outlying shopping mall would draw retail customers away from the downtown, destroying it, and leaving it a wasteland. Second, immense expenditure had gone into making the area work as a central business district and civic center over the years—its utility infrastructure, its traffic and transportation system, and its considerable service mechanisms. Third, the city would be obliged to spend millions of dollars on the outlying site for new sewers, water lines, and a custom-made parkway connection.

Faced with a proposition like this—and propositions of this kind are presented to cities all over America every day—mayors and council members seem to feel they are in the presence of a superior being, so ready are they to lose their virtue to the seducer. (Bribery is by no means the only impetus.) "Allow us," they seem to implore the developer, "to bring these brand new utilities and facilities right to the doorstep of this remote area and in addition grant you a significant abatement in local taxes for the next ten years!" The fact that a large increase in tax revenues is supposed to be a major local benefit of any such development is recklessly tossed aside during negotiations in fear of losing the developer. Is the planning director consulted in such a case? Probably not. And certainly not if he sounded even slightly tentative about the proposal when the mayor deigned to describe it on the telephone. Once the developer rolls into town, all discussions take place in mayor and council chambers in an orgy of blissful seduction and self-destruction, with plenty of technical assistance by the controller, corporation counsel, city engineer, traffic engineer, and budget director. After reading the high points of the plan in the local newspaper, however, the "uncooperative" local planner finds his calls to the mayor's office go unreturned.

In the case in question, however—somehow the local planner got her day in court. The city manager's office was stuffed with high-level political and technical personnel, related and unrelated to planning and development. The planner made a strong case for the industrial development of the site, emphasizing its need and viability as a light industrial park, giving as well all the cited reasons against its development as a shopping mall. At one point she said: "When they clash, we've got to separate developmental objectives from the objectives of increased revenues." Everybody laughed. (Everybody laughed!) To them, apparently, development was *for* revenues. It did not matter what development did to the city and to future generations, or if it did matter, it was not worth examining too carefully.

Most of the top administrative staff pushed hard for the outlying shopping mall proposal. But when it went before the city council, this body turned it down! This unexpected departure regaled the planning staff. Now, why would the city council suddenly turn it down after all that enthusiasm during the discussion process? I have no idea. The grapevine produced a rumor that individual council members did not get as much from the potential developer as they had anticipated.

The following fictitious letter from a frustrated local planner to a fictitious concerned citizen attempts to convey additional realities about the myth of the planner as a member of the local political team:

Dear Pub:
When you came in today and asked me what the "city's position" was on the Cloughlin site, I was disturbed, as I always am, when I hear that kind of question, because it so erroneously presupposes that all city personnel are of one mind. Why is it so hard for you concerned citizens to picture what it's like at City Hall? Is it so hard to imagine that we could be in disagreement? In point of fact, dear Pub, when my planning department is asked to give its opinion on a planning question, our opinion is often the reverse of that of elected officials.

But I can't share that fact with you. It would undoubtedly sound as if I thought the Mayor's opinion was ill-advised or motivated to bring in more real estate taxes which he could point to when the next election campaign rolled around, while my view is motivated for the good of the city and is therefore the correct, decent, honorable one (which is of course what I think). I am afraid that if I gave you my professional view, you would inadvertently spill the beans with your zeal, which could put me in bad with the Mayor, and that could (as frequently happens in such cases) result in my dismissal.

You probably think I am exaggerating, but the sad fact is that local politicians are always looking to fill jobs like mine with their political supporters. A purely professional planner, who is just in there to do her best for the whole city, who has no civil service or political ties—she is always expendable when political or financial pressures develop. We're just flapping around out there.

As you know, the Cloughlin site is one of the few open space sites left in the city. It is surrounded with detached houses on half-acre lots. There is a lot of pressure from the City Council and the Mayor to rezone it for high-rise apartments to accommodate a developer who has approached the city with plans for a very dense residential development. I can't just say to them that we need the open space and should therefore try to preserve it as a public park or open recreation area. That would cost the city dearly. A private group

might be found to use the estate as a private golf course, but that has
about a 2 percent chance of being realized. That might be the best
solution, because both sides of the issue would be getting a large
portion of what they want—open space and taxes.

But if I simply proposed that the city take over the estate as a
public park, I would lose a great deal of credibility with the city
council (credibility I definitely need to function here as a planner)
because of what they would see as my ignorance of the recreation
department's limited budget and of the need for additional city
revenues.

My staff and I are busily trying to prove with actual figures that
an increase in population of the magnitude proposed for the site
(schoolchildren, traffic, etc.) would shoot up city service costs so
much that it would nullify the higher real estate tax yield of the
development. When we have finished this research, the Mayor may
permit us to present it to the City Council in executive session. But
even if we get this opportunity, it may not be nearly enough. A staff
planner can fight only in a limited way when his views differ from
those of elected officials.

You, dear Pub, have got to help. Elected officials will pay attention to you, however reluctantly. All I can give you is information,
and I can give you plenty of that. To be effective, you will have to
put together a group, go before the Mayor and Council yourselves,
try to get some press attention, hand out leaflets, do whatever it
takes. Public outcry works. It is the only effort that does work
against greed, stupidity, and special interests.

Sincerely,
Your Local Planner

To be fair, occasionally local planners get deeply into political life. By
and large, however, either the city is financially sound and its problems relatively minor, producing almost no controversy as to appropriate
solutions, or the planner loses favor with the mayor following the first
serious disagreement, after which he is gradually frozen out. Even Allan
B. Jacobs reports in his generally affirmative work *Making City Planning
Work* that once he, as planning director of San Francisco, was out of
favor with the mayor, there was no going back to a team relationship.
Even under a "weak-mayor" form of government, a mayor can usually
find a way to brush aside the local planner. In San Francisco in 1973 more
and more city planning and related functions were undertaken by new
planners within the mayor's own office, starting with the new federally-
funded Office of Community Development. This threatening contrivance
succeeded, at least in part, in bringing about the resignation of this fully-
entrenched planning director within a relatively short time.[4]

THE MAYOR AND CITY COUNCIL AS
ENLIGHTENED STATESMEN MYTH

The multiplicity of volumes and essays published on urban planning is striking. And if elected city officials tend to shun planning scholarship in arriving at developmental decisions, one cannot help wondering who is reading these books. Behind most planning treatises seems to be the flagrant, persistent, and mistaken assumption that local elected officials base their developmental decisions on solid facts and good judgment—that they in fact search out the truth, that in this search they will turn to books by planners and university professors for help and guidance. This is called "the presumed readership syndrome." The truth is—with the possible exception of the few cosmopolitan cities in America—even superlative works like those of Lewis Mumford are rarely found on the bookshelves of local elected decision-makers. All those meticulously phrased, passionate descriptions, ideas, insights, and philosophical postulates about cities— unknown to the typical local decision-maker. As we have seen, Mumford was strongly opposed to high-density housing. Have the people who made density decisions for actual housing developments in the past thirty years read these passages? Are they even vaguely aware of the existence of Mumford's works? Indeed, the gulf between the urban political world and the great hordes of books on planning library shelves can be measured in light years.

Of course! You are thinking: the planner reads the books and enlightens the decision-makers. But the planner is not in a privileged position. She cannot freely walk into the mayor's office. She has to make an appointment with his secretary just like everyone else. And she has her hands full just getting a brief audience with the mayor for something she's pursuing. She can fight for relevant good ideas, but in this environment she cannot read aloud eloquent, thought-provoking passages. Probably she cannot even lend the mayor a planning book without insulting or annoying him.

Planning books are probably read by three types of persons: (1) their authors, (2) planning students, and (3) big readers—readers who read multitudes of anything and everything well-written and well-presented. Big readers will be impressed by good arguments found in planning books, but rarely will they communicate these points to local elected officials, whose paths they seldom cross, even by mail. The gulf widens.

Local elected officials are unenlightened in other ways. Because they must run for election every two or four years, they are not, as we have said, interested in long-term issues. They seem not to realize that if they fail to address long-term problems, there will be no empowered leader to fill this role, to everyone's peril.

The irony is that urban development is by its very nature fairly long-term. There is no such thing as a quick or short-term redevelopment program to which a new mayor can point before the next two-year election. Moreover, local politicans often do not understand developmental preliminaries—feasibility studies, pro formas, pragmatic rationales. They fail to recognize that the legal requirements of changing the use of an urban site can take a few years at best. Despite the incredible complexity of developmental issues, they want quick, simple solutions and magic-wand new construction.

Especially in a city that really needs help, one political party will not go ahead with a development project the other party started, not unless it is too far along to stop. After the public presentation of a detailed development plan in such a city, a local newspaper announced that even though political control of the city council had shifted in the recent election from the Democrats to the Republicans, "bipartisan support assures progress" on the development in question, "all parties agreed." (All parties agreed!) All parties were deluded if they agreed. There was absolutely no chance in a political, multi-problemed town like the one in question that the Republicans would build a Democratic plan, or vice versa. Why is this especially true in a city that has many problems? Enlightened, idealistic people will not get deeply involved in local politics when the city's problems seem to be insurmountable. Who fills the breach? All too often it is filled by people who see local politics as a means of exploitation and personal aggrandizement.

THE MYTH THAT EFFECTIVE LOCAL PLANNING CAN EASILY OCCUR IN AMERICAN CITIES

Real Estate

An immense impediment to success that American urban planners must face every day, in one form or another, comes under the heading of real estate—that category of business that reduces land and shelter to commodities, the primary purpose of which is the provision of profits. This is no overstatement. Any landlord or developer will staunchly defend this contention. By contrast, the committed planner views land and shelter as the solid environment of life, the primary purposes of which are habitation and enjoyment by living creatures.

In public agencies dealing with urban development, components of these opposing views are perpetually in play, as if tossed in the air by a juggler. Despite zoning laws, good and bad, the entrepreneurial view of land and shelter always prevails when there is any real contest, despite occasional heroic counterefforts by idealists. Boards of zoning appeals can grant variances; zoning maps can be changed. And rare is the zoning map that represents an idealistic plan in any case, one that dares, for instance, to call for a new park in an overly built-up area. (Ask any Manhattan real estate entrepreneur what he thinks about Central Park, for instance. He will tell you: "It's just crazy to leave all that valuable land lying open when it could be bringing in mountains of rents and revenues!")

I am not referring here to the real estate agent who helps people buy and sell houses. Real estate agents fulfill an important and useful function, as we all know. I am referring to the whole financial, taxation, and legal system of real property that has distorted the meaning of land "value" to a great degree. In real estate terms the "highest and best use" of a site is the use that will yield the highest price per square foot—the highest rent, resale price, or taxes. Local taxes are of course based on land value; land value is based on market value; and market value is the dollar amount an owner can get for a piece of property put up for sale. In real estate's value system a hot dog stand shaped like a hot dog (I saw one in the Colorado Rocky Mountains) is "improved" land. Any developed piece of a land is "improved." Conversely, a beautiful pastoral place is dubbed "unimproved" land!

The most injurious aspect of the domination of the real estate view of land and shelter is the local taxation of property according to market value or profit yield. Real estate taxation makes local planning exceedingly difficult, if not impossible. The land use that is best for the people, the neighborhood, or the community is considered secondarily, if at all, by typical elected officials. An appropriate use for a site from the community viewpoint often pays less in taxes than a poor one. Mayors and city councils therefore opt for the use that pays the highest revenues. Fortunate is the planner who is promoting a development project that also pays high taxes.

For decades various scholars have recommended that local governments tap revenue sources other than the property tax, but this reform apparently has few powerful proponents. Nevertheless, with local taxes based on different elements, such as individual income, value added in business, and/or payrolls, decisions affecting local land and shelter could be based on community issues alone, devoid of the false and compromising revenue motive.

Local planners wanting to be involved in private developmental decision-making must work with real estate developers. We are unequivocally in bed with the enemy. Confident of their supremacy in the entire land system, developers try to straighten out "the muddle-headed thinking" of local planners every step of the way. If the planners mount any opposition to the developers' proposals, they are simply bypassed as superfluous. The developers are thereafter free to deal directly with the building commissioner and other cooperative personnel.

Invariably, when the developer introduces a proposal to the city, he brings along a beautiful architectural rendering and specifications that are attractive from all viewpoints. Local decisions are then made on the basis of these introductory submissions. Frequently, however, months later when the project is ready to go, "financial realities force" the developer to cut ambiance and amenities to the bone. With elected officials having already gone too far to turn back, in most cases, the final, utilitarian design bears little resemblance to the beautiful original proposal. Sound familiar? I would venture a guess that it happens in an American city every day.

This pattern of operations is not true of James Rouse, the developer of such marvelous festival marketplaces as Quincy Market in Boston and Harborplace in Baltimore. He is unique. James Rouse is indeed a national treasure.

The perverse mentality of all too many developers was demonstrated in a classic case in which a city's zoning authorities thought they had prevented any skyscraper construction in a downtown zone by stipulating that total floor space in any new buildings not exceed fourteen times the site's area. But a developer outsmarted them by assembling seven parcels into one huge lot, building a soaring skyscraper that blocked one of the city's loveliest views and set dangerous precedents. In other words, the people's elected officials had passed a law precisely to prevent skyscraper development in this location, for the benefit of the community, and this law was deliberately circumvented by the developer.

Indisputably, planners have to know about real estate, know about the private sector, know development financing, and understand local politics. These are some of the tools of our trade, after all. But knowing about things does not mean becoming them, does not mean devoting oneself to their goals. A motivated city planner keeps faith with his own goal of maximum community benefit. He lets other participants in the urban development world know that his goals are different from theirs, even though the legal system bases most property laws on the market and income-value of land and property.

This is not to infer that it makes sense to study urban planning in the late twentieth century. Some universities are apparently teaching planning today as a set of skills, like typing, shorthand, and bookkeeping, not as a profession with a mission. Mired in self-serving obfuscation and confusion, too many of today's planners and urban experts seem to have convinced themselves that because city planning and real estate deal with the same subjects, their pursuits are interchangeable. Obsequious evidence of this thinking comes across one's desk every week. Real estate and city planning deal with land and property from opposing objectives. It is pure deception and fantasy to attempt to blend these two in the unctuous and disingenuous manner that is frequently employed by urban organizations.

Harborplace in Baltimore, aerial view
(Courtesy of the Rouse Company)

Harborplace in Baltimore
(Courtesy of the Rouse Company)

Money and Programs

One of the greatest obstacles to effective urban planning is, of course, the outrageous inadequacy of public funding for urban improvement and housing in the late twentieth century. That goes without saying. In relation to the need, these problems are merely thrown a few bones.

When funding *is* available, another major obstacle is the "program" approach to governmental solutions, instead of the sustained, ongoing effort that is so greatly needed. Sadly, the grandest federal solutions ever instituted for curing urban problems—those introduced or reconstructed by President Kennedy's New Frontier or President Johnson's Great Society— had serious defects in this respect. The Great Society's *Catalog of Federal Assistance Programs* of 1967 briefly describes (one to a page) 459 social, economic, and building programs. If my experience with these programs was illustrative, it was not unusual for a program to contain at least one technical flaw that made it well-nigh unworkable—like a mortgage program that required the voluntary assistance of banks but set interest rates 0.25 percent below conventional mortgages. Another problem with these programs was that many did not address fundamentals; they attempted to treat end results without correcting root causes. And the duration of many of the programs was entirely too short. Programs, programs, programs. Eighteen-month prescriptions for century-old ailments. Some became in effect demonstration programs that "proved" to the public that "nothing could be done" when the truth lay in the fact that decades of help were needed before the relevant societal ailments could be cured.

In a society motivated largely by money, that views land and shelter primarily as real estate, it is amazing that such an extraordinary effort was made by these 1960s administrations. But it takes one or two generations of sustained effort, with patience and adjustment all the way along, to correct most of our urban problems, especially social problems that are rooted in the past. In their short life, the New Frontier/Great Society programs demonstrated what might well work and what probably would not. Most of all they proved that more time was needed, within a steady, on-going, well-funded system.

Tax-Sharing

Obstacles to planning effectuation can stem from excessive home rule chauvinism. A case in point is the perpetual attempt by the typical local government to bring profitable retail development to its own jurisdiction, no matter what—a preoccupation tragically common throughout much of the country. The root cause of this mad desire is of course real estate and sales taxes. No argument there. It follows that if City A could accumulate as much in net taxes from a new retail development located in nearby City B as it could from one developed within its own borders, its local government would be satisfied. It is a logical idea that is not pursued, to my knowledge, even by regional planning agencies. Under such a tax-sharing system all the municipalities in a retailing region would benefit from the expansive retail development of the city most appropriate to this development from the planning point of view: broad-market-area location, radial transportation network, and the like.

Although it is vitally important for retail and office facilities to be concentrated in centers capable of servicing a large area, it is equally important to create a workable tax-sharing system that permits the cities and towns left out of the development picture to profit from such concentrated business development. This may be the only way cities and towns will stop reaching out for inappropriate, taxable projects slated for location almost anywhere within their borders, at almost any cost.

Legal Empowerment of Planners

These are just a few examples of the massive planning implementational drought in America. Other examples permeate this work. By far the gravest obstacle is the planners' lack of power in law, as described in Chapter 1. It sounds fine and logical for elected officials to have the final word in all local decisions. But it is not. There needs to be a strong mechanism whereby the local planner can disapprove inappropriate development, pursue unpopular solutions to grave problems, address long-term issues, and work as a respected, legally-empowered member of the local management team.

NOTES

1. Allan B. Jacobs, *Making City Planning Work* (Washington, DC/Chicago: American Planning Association, 1980), p. 179.

2. Thomas Adams, *Outline of Town and City Planning*, pp. 213, 327.

3. Stanford Environmental Law Society, "Castration of Zoning," *Cry California* (Fall 1970), pp. 18-19. (This short article from the *San Jose Land Use Study* is an inset within Karl Belser's article "The Making of Slurban American," previously cited.)

4. Jacobs, *Making City Planning Work*, pp. 256-73.

6

Obstructionists

Because planners have so little to do with actual urban development, many evolve into other entities. Unfortunately they continue to use the professional designation of *planner*, even though they have passed through various kinds of transformation. By interfering directly or indirectly with pragmatic action-oriented planners, or by supplanting them, these planners have become *obstructionists*. All eleven types bring dishonor to the profession. It should be noted that this series of transformations was first observed during the century's most active planning and renewal period, 1949-1973. Today obstructionists undoubtedly predominate among planners.

The *suspensionist* is a planner devoid of a sense of urgency. He sees the city as static. In his mind all human life within his purview is *suspended* while he takes his time in arriving at solutions and approving vital projects. By his actions, he apparently assumes that if he does not get around to helping the children living in a certain area before they grow up, perhaps he will help their children or grandchildren. But nothing is to be done until all the bugs are out of his plan. By that time, the plan is out of date and must be revised.

To the suspensionist time stands still. His evil lies primarily in the loss of time in making real-world improvements. The living and breathing citizenry, some of whom are small children who cannot grow up normally or comfortably in urban slums, whose adult lives can therefore be irreparably damaged, these children and those that follow must wait for decades for the improvements they need. The suspensionist's harm is packaged both in time lost and in bringing disfavor to the profession by his seemingly innocent irresponsibility and lack of reality.

Dennis O'Harrow would recognize the suspensionist as one of those planners who view the plan as an ideal you are not supposed to achieve, a guide to what the city would look like if the plan were implemented, which it never is.[1]

The *projectionist* first came to mind at an all-day conference in New York at which a former professor of mine, one of the most intelligent and well-respected planners in America, devoted a speech to the demographic and economic trends that were continuing to damage cities. He projected that these trends would continue over the next two decades. I waited for the word "unless"—"unless sound planning policies are undertaken," for instance. But there was not one qualification in his speech. He prophesized doom and that was it—more and more of the middle class moving to the suburbs, more rural poor migrating to the cities, the ruination of the railroads, the overexpenditure of public funds on automobile travel, and the proliferation of outlying shopping centers. All at once this erstwhile stalwart was not a planner anymore. He was a projectionist. He simply gave his projections and terminated his speech. It was almost as if he thought the situation was hopeless. Certainly it was well-nigh hopeless if one of our leading planners was not even going to outline the steps that could be taken to offset these trends, however radical or unlikely of achievement.

Projectionists produce copious studies, reports, and analyses of prospects for cities, addressing population change, income, age, migration to the suburbs, and occupations based on present market trends. Their forecasts never identify city planning as a potential protagonist for altering the scenario. They are usually intelligent people, but they refuse to urge the enlightened population to forestall or reverse dire trends.

Then there are the *metamorphists*. In local planning and development agencies, a gradual metamorphosis loses to the ranks of committed idealism honest (but gullible) city planners who originally entered the public service with the hope of effecting great urban improvements. A metamorphist invariably begins to change with her "discovery" of the fantastic and overwhelming "realities" of a developer's legal and fiscal problems. Her loss to planning and the public is the developer's gain, for she unwittingly transforms herself into a developer's advocate. The metamorphist becomes proficient in the needs and demands of the marketplace, struggling to make something happen virtually to the exclusion of concern for the needs of the people to be served or for the objectives of the development plan. As in all cases of pure naiveté, the metamorphist's transformation usually occurs despite the total absence of any factual knowledge of the developer's assets or percentage of profits. It often develops to the point that the metamorphist virtually takes on the objectives of the entrepreneur herself, entirely without personal gain. Metamorphism tends to be infectious; it feels so good to be respected for one's astute grasp of the situation, and other planners can sense that. Gradually, during moments of agency decision-making, true planning voices—those promoting maximum community benefit—become fewer and fewer.

Next we have the *accommodators*. In the position of local planning director, the accommodator foresakes his own judgment or creative thought as a basis for making recommendations in order to establish compatible relations with the mayor or city manager. Clearly all local planning must work *through* elected officials. Every zoning ordinance, every urban renewal project, every community development project must be approved by the city council or other legislative body and administered by the mayor or other chief executive. But to quality as a bona fide professional, a planning director must propose to these elected officials what he considers to be good solutions and attempt to discourage bad ones, even if his advice is sometimes proffered privately. He must support his professional views with factual analyses, as well as provide technical assistance. The accommodator, on the other hand, yields all decision-making to local elected officials. His endorsement, deftly rationalized as his own proposal for the benefit of the local citizens group, is provided for whatever these officials want to do. Technical assistance prevails. This total abdication of influence assures him of a job with the city for many years and through many administrations. He is able to reside for decades in the same community, his wife is able to keep her friends, and his children can remain in the same school. It is probably not an exaggeration to state that any city's long-term planning director may well be an accommodator, because the very nature of local planning is such that replacement of a bona fide planner after a few years is inevitable as the result of conceptual clashes or local elections. This is a sad fact of American city planning that I do not dismiss lightly; but one wonders if this reality can justify absolute abandonment of professional integrity.

The *confusionist* often teaches and publishes. She deliberately clouds issues with euphemisms, irrelevancies, planning gobbeldygook, technocratic time wasting, and perpetuation of the myths, often disparate, of the planner's role, functions, methods, scope, and tools. She is preoccupied with city planning as an academic mystique which she apparently believes will endure despite the ignorance of its very existence in real-world developmental change. Countless numbers of words are published each month by confusionists in professional journals and hard cover volumes, barely a word of which ever reaches the eyes of the general public or their elected officials. If ever there was a professional offshoot that talks to itself, in numerous, voluminous publications and editions, that offshoot is confusionism.

This deliberate confusion is no small handicap to urban improvement. Not only is it a waste of time and resources, it so disturbs the reform-oriented planners that they feel obliged out of conscience to spend their valuable time attempting to clarify the obvious in speeches and articles. The confusionist unceasingly requires a definition, or redefinition, of planning. Is planning an end? Is it a process? Is it a guide to implementation? What is implementation? "Do I dare to eat a peach?"[2]

In a book review of a 1,166-page collection of articles by planners and other urban experts, audaciously entitled *Taming Megalopolis*, Clive Entwistle observes that the authors "tame" megalopolis about the way a mouse "drives" an elephant it has caught a ride upon:

> There is a Sufi teaching story about a mouse that climbed onto the head of an elephant and imagined himself to be its mahout [driver]. To preserve the illusion of control the mouse-mahout programmed his commands to follow the movements of the great beast, which was, of course, unaware of his presence. It is in this nursery sense only that the title "Taming Megalopolis" can be applied to these two volumes of papers by some 65, mainly academic, experts in the fields of urban sociology, economics and planning. . . .
>
> [The term megalopolis] was coined by Jean Gottman in 1961 to describe the vast urban and suburban conglomeration that sprawls over some 500 miles of the northeast seaboard. The present habitat of some 40-million Americans, it is still expanding, at an increasing rate, without benefit of conscious control, direction or evaluation. . . .
>
> It is frustrating to discover that any decision maker seeking comprehensive guidelines to action in these volumes would be quite disappointed. Indeed, he would feel an intruder in these generally precious pages. . . .
>
> Not only does the urban expert refrain from positive prescription. He actively tends, in his efforts to adapt his commands to the imponderable movements of the megalopolitan elephant, to negate and paralyze valid action programs already begun by men of simpler natures.[3]

Then we have the *satisfactionist*. He is muddle-headed and has a very poor sense of relative values. First he is satisfied with the limited planning "tools" in America, the means of implementing city planning: usually zoning, subdivision or site plan regulations, housing code enforcement, and urban redevelopment. Similarly he is content with the planner's assortment of professional concerns—the components of "city planning" that have been tacked on, as we have seen, one by one since the late nineteenth century, but that remain incomplete and disjointed to this day—civic design, land use planning, population studies, local economic base, subdivision planning, slum clearance, environment, and so on. The satisfactionist is also content with the well-known paper planning that has no effect on local government decision-making, and finally, he is satisfied with tiny real-world achievements, such as the renovation of one small block of tenements within a huge devastated ghetto.

In a word, the satisfactionist is complacent. Within the ambiguous context of his daily lack of true successes, he tends to misjudge the value of these scraps, likening them to major, influential accomplishments. This mental state is followed by total relaxation of whatever zeal he may ever have had.

Next we have the *ingenuist*, who claims or implies that urban problems are actually "corrected" with rational planning and that planners are in the midst of the fray and getting results. As excellent examples of ingenuistic prose, two paragraphs are quoted below from the 1959 edition of the only overall textbook on city planning that existed in America between 1959 and 1968, *Local Planning Administration*. The introductory chapter, from which these excerpts are taken, was written by a member of the American Institute of Planners (now AICP) under the heading "Scope of City Planning":

> Various mechanisms operate to keep a complex urban structure functioning. One is the economic system which, through the medium of land values, rents, construction costs, and the like, helps to direct community development into certain channels. But economic forces cannot always be depended upon to bring about a socially desirable community pattern. Hence they must be supplemented by application of foresight and planned administrative and legal coordination if balance, harmony, and order are to be ensured. It is the task of city planning to supply this foresight and this over-all coordination.[4]

This last sentence gives the impression that "overall coordination" of "economic forces" is a relatively small hurdle for the city planner. But local elected officials do not think the planning director knows any more about economic forces than they do. If the planning director even gets an audience with the mayor on such matters, in person or in writing, it usually means he has fought hard for such an advantage through the careful employment of diplomacy, psychology, and the other puny devices available to a committed American planner. But to get the elected officials to follow his economic advice when they disagree is a virtual impossibility.

Also under "Scope of City Planning," this planner's words of indoctrination make it seem as if city planners are deeply involved in urban development:

> The process of applying foresight and coordination to the location,

extent, and timing of public and private improvements in order to prevent or minimize maladjustments, defects, and deficiencies is what is meant by city planning. The process of guiding this continual adjustment is the basic and distinctive function of the planning agency. Through it the planning agency aims to ensure that each new improvement helps transform the present community into a better one.[5]

The implication conveyed in this paragraph is that the local planning director is (1) automatically informed of "each new improvement" in the preliminary stages and (2) permitted to interfere in a developer's development process with respect to a certain local site. Nothing could be further from the truth. In a typical city, a prospective developer can easily investigate the zoning of a piece of property by going to the local building department and obtaining copies of the zoning ordinance and building code. He may then obtain an option on the property while his plans are drawn up. If his plans meet these legal requirements, he receives a building permit from the building department. In many cities the planning director is not part of this process. If the building commissioner is not predisposed to involve the planning director, nor instructed by the mayor to do so, he is not failing in his duty when he proceeds on his own. It would not be unusual for a local planning director to hear of a proposed development for the first time through the local newspaper or by the personal observation of a bulldozer working on the site.

In the event that a developer wants to develop something that is not permitted under the zoning, which is very common, he may have to request a variance from the board of zoning appeals. If the city council or the mayor or both desire this new development (and chances are they will), it will be granted, for the city council frequently has the power to override the recommendations of the board of zoning appeals. The usual reasons for the administration's wanting a proposed development are (1) tax revenues, (2) jobs, and (3) "progress." In corrupt cities, developers bribe the mayor or council to do their bidding.

Getting back to the ingenuistic utterances at hand, not only is there very little "guiding" by the planning director of the "continual adjustment" or of the "location, extent, and timing" of private improvements, the planner's voice, as we have seen, is typically paid no more attention to than that of others in the administration—the corporation counsel, the chief engineer, the comptroller, the traffic engineer, the public works director, the building commissioner, or the sanitation director.

This planner undoubtedly meant no harm, but in my opinion it is unjustifiable to make claims of this sort in a basic text on planning. It is harmful to encourage people who are considering entrance into a profession to believe that it functions effectively and possesses authority it does not possess.

The *accumulator* is a planning researcher who cannot stop collecting data. Dealing with a universe as complex as a city obviously requires a great deal of research. Considerable data collection is necessary also to describe and characterize a district or neighborhood, and computers can be of remarkable assistance here. But fascination with the mystique of data collection and with the mental gymnastics of correcting its imperfections—combined with fear of incorrect solutions and poor judgment—often produce over-researching of known elements or elements about which the conventional wisdom is close enough for the purposes intended. The accumulator's poor judgment is manifested in not being able to make these distinctions.

A perfect example of an accumulator's handiwork is the community renewal program for a major city that cost several millions of dollars and was to take six months. The planning department of this metropolis got extensively involved in computer data collection, had difficulty perfecting the methods, and ended up with a rehash of census data. Four years after starting, the department produced a thin little document describing what everybody already knew about the city, that is, everybody over the age of twelve who could read and write.

Next we have the *mathematical modelers*. These Ph.D. planners have cajoled the foundations and universities into spending thousands of dollars and time on perfecting the computer for *planning decision-making*. Buried deep within almost incomprehensible jargon, their journal articles have been known to admit that mathematical modeling fails when it comes to providing solutions to problems that are not innately quantifiable. Solutions to many urban problems are not numerical. Therefore if a computer is to be used, nonnumerical entities must be "assigned" or "allocated" numbers, and this assignment requires human judgment, which the computer does not possess. In addition, assumptions ("predetermined criteria" in the jargon of the modelers) must be made by human brains before they are programmed into the computer. What the computer does is greatly simplify mathematical processes. It is, for example, enormously useful in the comparison of various quantifiable alternative courses of action in the areas of traffic, transportation, and public utilties.

A classic example of the folly and waste of money and time by the mathematical modelers was found in a regional transportation plan for a northeastern metropolitan area that cost millions of dollars and took ten years to complete. I have it on good authority from erstwhile staff members that so many problems were caused by the attempt to use the computer *for planning* that much time was spent in trying to correct the computer's errors. At one point in the project, whole towns were "eliminated" by the computer. Human fudging ("innocent deception") was used to correct these errors, which were built upon, subsequently, in further analyses. Validity was compromised.

Bureaucrats in planning think nothing of putting ease of work and high salaries above service. Among them the practice of leaving a job after only one year for higher pay is common when jobs are plentiful. As it takes at least a year to get to know a city, the contribution to a community during so short a time is negligible.

Bureaucracy might be described as public service employment for the wrong reasons. It is fatal to effective planning. Civil service for professional workers usually turns out to be no less of a hindrance to creative productive service than patronage and the spoils system (although sadly it may be imperative for the continued employment of older and minority planners who are the first to be laid off in a budget crunch).

In bureaucratic city planning seldom does a two-year study ever end; in eras of prosperity extensions are always asked for and granted. Parkinson's law is employed to keep one's job. To stay on requires (1) the "building of an empire" of civil service drones, and (2) the "making of no waves" to upset local politicians, bringing attention to the erstwhile temporary unit.

The law of diminishing returns operates here also, and one's greatest concern in such a situation becomes *not* the solution of a community's problem but the concern of how many staff members, and which ones, should receive copies of such and such a memo.

Bureaucrats in planning do not wear the mantle of evil; their appearance is not menacing. They are frequently nice people; they have families. It is not easy, therefore, for a mayor, who must always run scared from election to election, to take the risk of weeding them out to get something done. A mayor eager to make a difference may simply let the drones stay on, introducing an additional group capable of performing. Even here, in time, the displaced bureaucrats can hinder the new group's work with demands for rights of review.

Meyerson and Banfield may have been thinking in part of bureaucrats when they made the following devastating observation:

> Some people are temperamentally incapable of reflection, of dealing with the larger aspects of matters, of seeing the elements of a situation in their mutual relations, or of viewing affairs in a long perspective of time. Although they may be poorly qualified, temperamentally, for planning these people are sometimes in charge of planning agencies or staffs. There is, in fact, a natural selection which tends to fill top planning posts with such people.[6]

Finally, we have the *deletoid*. Disingenuous to a fault, the deletoid's pernicious method of planning is to report only a portion of the truth about a city and to recommend solutions for only portions of its ills, probably because she knows the political leaders do not want the entire story to be told. Having an inactive sense of mission to the general public, she favors whatever the politicians want her to favor and backs up proposals with empty facts and planning jargon.

Consulting work in a northeastern city in 1966 provided me with what appeared to be a perfect paradigm of deletoid planning. A community action organization asked me to look into the need for improved housing and other neighborhood facilities in six blighted neighborhoods in this city of over 150,000 people. Briefly put, I found these six neighborhoods to be horrifyingly blighted, perhaps the worst I had ever seen, and I found the *Master Plan of Land Use*, which had been adopted by the local planning commission in 1962, to contain (1) insufficient identification of the horrendous condition of these neighborhoods and (2) no solutions at all for their correction. Following is a physical description of the six areas I prepared at the time:

> The virtual absence of any kind of pleasant physical environment in these neighborhoods is dramatic indeed. It is . . . not enough to improve the health, psychological, educational, and employment conditions of the slum residents' lives without also improving the physical neighborhoods. The extent to which the public housing has deteriorated is remarkable. Visually the neighborhoods have a broken, crumbling, and patched appearance, with curbs, sidewalks, foundations, building walls for the most part left unrepaired. In my opinion, the environment of these neighborhoods is gloomy, bleak, and capable of causing extreme despair among those who are unable to move to better neighborhoods.

According to the 1960 census, 22 percent of the families in the six blighted neighborhoods in question earned less than $3,000 a year (very low income even then), and 46 percent earned less than $5,000. ($6,000 was then considered the lower limit of "middle income.") Twenty-two percent of the dwelling units in these neighborhoods were substandard. The city may have had at the time the largest proportion of public housing units in the country. Out of a total of 51,654 dwelling units, 3,869 were in public housing, 3,563 of which were located in these six neighborhoods. Although 1960 was a time of prosperity, 8.9 percent of those living in the six neighborhoods were unemployed, and of the 25-year-olds and older living there, 34 percent had not completed eighth grade. Social problems, therefore, matched very closely the dreadful physical conditions of the selected neighborhoods. I discovered that the average middle-income resident of this city rarely saw these areas. It is laid out in such a way that it is easy for middle-income citizens to avoid seeing these derelict neighborhoods in conducting their daily lives.

Under the heading "Goals for Growth," the city's *Master Plan of Land*

Use provides the following statement under "Apartment Development:"

The first of these goals is the establishment of diversified population elements within the city. The plan should provide a physical basis for a population which reflects all income levels present in the region. In order to accomplish this, the city's land development policy should be geared to encourage the construction of modern housing facilities suitable to meet the demand of the middle and upper income families which it is now losing. Specifically, it must be geared to providing modern residential facilities such as garden apartments, town houses and high-rise apartments in areas where present housing is obsolete. *In addition, provision should be made for an ample supply of sound housing for lower income groups.* (Italics supplied)

This kind of reference to low-income housing provision, if not amplified with firm recommendations for specific amounts and types of housing, is pure lip service. No proposals are made for improved housing for low-income groups per se in the "Summary of Major Plan Objectives," which stresses the need for modern apartment development, new industrial sites, shopping facilities, and improvement of the central business district. Under a detailed discussion of housing needs the plan emphasizes the city's deficiency in relatively small-sized apartments—"higher priced," "quality rental housing"—but it includes no discussion at all of low-rent housing needs. (I should point out here that I am not opposed to trying to attract middle-income back to a city; in fact, I believe a substantial middle-income group is essential to a healthy city. The point is that horrendous conditions existed that were ignored or glossed over in the master plan for the entire city.) The sole reference to the provision of standard housing for low-income groups is the one sentence quoted and italicized above. Thus the six neighborhoods that I found so terrible as physical environments were invisible when it came to recommended improvements.

With respect to identification of problems, all the city's neighborhoods are described in the plan's Appendix entitled "Neighborhood Analysis/ Profile." Neighborhood No. 4, probably the worst of the six neighborhoods, contained a massive public housing project of 1,239 dwelling units, built in 1940. Crime was so high in this project in the early 1960s that it was decided that something must be done about it. The city's solution was to put a highway right through the middle "in order to police the project better," I was told. According to the 1960 census, 31 percent of Neighborhood No. 4's housing units were substandard, assuming that the public housing units were standard, a doubtful assumption. Forty-six percent of the population was 18 years of age or under; in other words, almost half the residents were children. Broken homes were twice the city

average. Forty percent of family incomes were below $3,000. (Forty per-
cent!) Forty-eight percent of 25-year-olds and over did not progress to the
eighth grade. The Master Plan's Neighborhood Analysis/Profile of Neighborhood No. 4 is quoted below as an example of the plan's characterization
of an extremely blighted area. (Identifying proper names are edited out.)
What I want the reader to notice is the banality in the choice of concerns:

Land Uses

> HOUSING: Two- to six-family structures of older type, very
> rundown, lacking yards, parking and sanitary facilities; and
> . . . a public housing project.

> COMMERCIAL: Concentrated along East Main Street and
> . . . Avenue in old mixed-use structures, many rundown, offer-
> ing mostly local convenience goods with some secondary goods
> on East Main Street, lacking off-street parking and loading.

> INDUSTRIAL: Various small manufacturing concerns border
> the west side of the neighborhood, generally in older buildings
> occupying over 80 percent of their site area, cramped for park-
> ing and loading facilities.

Community Facilities

> SCHOOLS: . . . School, very old and very rundown.

> PLAYGROUNDS: One small play yard at the school, with no
> facilities; . . . Street playground, offering preschool children
> facilities and basketball courts, rundown and very dusty.

> PARKS: No nearby parks, neighborhood must depend upon its
> internal recreation system.

Traffic

> Heavy traffic exists along East Main Street and . . . Avenue;
> industrial trucking tends to penetrate local streets.

Blight Factors

> Very old housing, rundown; 100 percent lot coverage, little set-
> back along major traffic arteries, no off-street parking, industrial
> noise especially along the western edge, marginal and rundown
> commercial facilities, many commercial vacancies, lack of ade-
> quate recreation facilities, highway noise in the south part of the
> neighborhood, railroad noise along the north edge of the neigh-
> borhood, trucking on residential streets and southern portion of
> neighborhood severed by . . . (an expressway).

Present Land Use Plan

Continues multi-family residential throughout, and restricts commercial facilities to local shopping within . . . (public housing project) and along . . . Street, and secondary commercial and business district along East Main Street. Location of secondary shopping on East Main Street is questionable in view of secondary shopping two blocks to the north in Neighborhood Ten.

Present Zoning

Zoning does not conform to Land Use Plan. Allows light industrial throughout about 70 percent of the neighborhood, the rest being three types of residential densities. No provision is made for commercial facilities.

Setbacks, lot coverage, "rundown" housing, heavy traffic? These terms did not begin to describe the devastating characteristics of this area, yet a footnote states that "Blight factors are considered to be those physical characteristics of neighborhood environment which may eventually hasten the decline of an area. The presence of these factors does not necessarily indicate that the decline has already begun."

This type of neighborhood profile tells us nothing about the atmosphere, the character of the area, the typical lives of the people—the health conditions, police and fire calls, kinds of crimes, or drug traffic. Nothing about crumbling masonry, broken sidewalks, smashed ash cans, broken glass, derelict cars, horrendous smells, total absence of greenery, lack of light and air in apartments, overcrowding, strewn garbage, or old mattresses left lying in the rain. Indeed, photographs alone would have provided a profile of substantially greater accuracy than the verbal characterization contained in this plan.

To dramatize the inadequacy of this type of "analysis/profile," I present herewith a brief description of a well-known dreadful environment, based on eyewitness accounts, followed by a description of this place using the terminolgy of the referenced *Master Plan of Land Use*:

Newgate Gaol, a prison used in London between 1188 and 1902, had the following characteristics: perpetual darkness, perpetual cold in winter, excessive noise and clamor, incredible overcrowding, pervasive stench, heavily polluted air, vermin, near starvation for the poor, faulty sanitation, a thoroughly unhygienic atmosphere, rampant disease, frequent deaths, drinking, gaming, sexual orgies, nothing but bare ground to sit or lie upon, physical cruelty (bolts and shackles), constant horror and despair.[7]

**Newgate Gaol à la Referenced Master Plan of Land Use,
(1962) Neighborhood Analysis/Profiles**

Housing

> Communal housing facilities, very run down, lacking yards,
> services and sanitation facilities.

Traffic

> Heavy pedestrian traffic extends along the main corridors and
> penetrates local corridors.

Blight Factors

> Very old prison building, run down. 100% lot coverage; little
> setback along major arteries; no off-street parking; lack of ade-
> quate recreational facilities; societal noise, especially in the
> common areas; carriage noise along the western edge; wagon
> noise along the southern side; marginal nutritional facilities;
> many commercial vacancies.

Recreation

> The prison must depend upon its internal recreational system.

Not only do these eleven obstructionists to varying degrees prevent bona
fide planners from functioning, not only do they discourage good candidates from entering the field, they also bring contempt to the profession.

NOTES

1. Dennis O'Harrow, *ASPO Newsletter*, August 1967, p. 2 (newsletter of the
erstwhile American Society of Planning Officials).

2. T. S. Eliot, "The Love Song of J. Alfred Prufrock," *Poems* (New York: Alfred
A. Knopf, 1920), p. 42.

3. Clive Entwistle, "Total Habitat," The *New York Times Book Review* (December 31, 1967), pp. 1, 18, 19.

4. Mary McLean, ed., *Local Planning Administration*, 3d ed. (Chicago: International City Manager's Association, 1959), p. 10.

5. Ibid.

6. Meyerson and Banfield, *Politics, Planning*, p. 277.

7. Anthony Babington, *The English Bastille* (New York: St. Martin's Press, 1971).

7

Urban Redevelopment

Urban redevelopment involves the demolition of existing development and the construction of new development in its place. It is a very important process in (1) preserving natural land and (2) in providing something dramatic and pivotal that will spin off other improvements, sometimes rescuing a city's entire economy.

The term urban renewal, as used in this country in the 1950s and 1960s, included rehabilitation and conservation of existing properties along with redevelopment. This chapter focuses primarily on redevelopment, with special emphasis on redevelopment as a technique. Although the benefits of rehabilitation and conservation are indisputable, they are amply described in other works, including a few written by the author, as listed in the bibliography.

Federally-aided urban redevelopment in this country had an interesting and vital history. Its lifespan was 1949-73. Through Title I of the U.S. Housing Act of 1949 and subsequent amendments, cities were able to purchase privately-owned blighted land and change the land use completely. This could be accomplished within three to four years. Thus as a method of expeditious implementation of city planning, no other technique came close. A few of its significant marvels and flaws are discussed in Chapter 3.

Redevelopment has as its legal basis the power of eminent domain under which a city can condemn a property and pay the existing owner the court-determined price if he has refused to sell to the local agency or could not agree on a price through negotiation. Eminent domain amounts to fully remunerated confiscation. Zoning's legal basis is the police power; it tells the existing owner what he may and may not do with his property.

Zoning leaves ownership in existing hands and provides no financial compensation. (Owners have been known to be happier if the local agency buys their properties at a fair price, rather than zone them out, potentially lowering market value.) The power of eminent domain came into existence in Britain when it became necessary for the government forcibly to purchase land in order to lay roads through the countryside after owners had refused to sell for this obvious public purpose.

Indeed, a fundamental requirement of the law of eminent domain is its public-purpose requirement. The public purpose identified by Congress for Title I urban redevelopment was slum clearance. Probably the public purpose should have been the economic survival of cities, coupled with the rehousing of slum families. Another bona fide public purpose would have been that of preventing the continuous development of what is left of natural land within urban communities.

Procedures of the Title I urban renewal program may be summarized as follows: The cities requested funds from the U.S. Department of Housing and Urban Development to assist them with the renewal of certain project areas of varying size. Before this could be done, the state had to grant the municipality the power of eminent domain. The city could then require property owners within a specified urban renewal area to sell their properties to the city at "fair market value." Although many properties were not purchased and many others were bought by the city through negotiation, the power of eminent domain made it possible for the city to create a coherent, well-planned neighborhood, unhampered by the inevitable few property owners unwilling to sell at any price. Before the city could begin, it had to prove to the federal and state authorities that the project had been properly planned and programmed. The federal government supplied funds for this purpose.

Special kinds of mortgage financing were available to property owners under Title I. Moreover, municipalities could pay their share of renewal costs (either one-third or one-sixth) through the installation of municipal improvements, including those that would have been undertaken in any case. The federal government paid all other renewal costs. By far the largest cost item was the difference between the price paid for the slum properties and the lower resale price of cleared land to redevelopers for a new use, the "write-down." This was the primary incentive used to induce private developers to buy and build according to the new plan. Where urban redevelopment was located close to or became an integral part of a standard area, it met with much success in cities all over the country.

Criticism of urban renewal was abundant virtually from the start—accusations of a "bulldozer approach," "urban removal" in which the poor lost their homes and even their neighborhoods, a policy that favored the rich, and so on. I think it is fair to say that it is impossible to develop an entrepreneurial program that at least a few vultures will not exploit. But safeguards can to some extent be built into the process (and were) to prevent excesses. Incredibly, there were very few cases of corruption of the Title I urban renewal program during its entire existence, nation-wide. Indeed, in relation to the amount of money involved, the extent of wrongdoing was infinitesimal.

New low-income public housing should have been a concomitant part of urban renewal, even where the vacancy ratio of existing low-income housing was relatively high. Attractive new construction should have been available to people forced to move on a one-for-one basis, demoli-tion to new construction. This would have reduced the onus of urban removal and added to the always much-needed supply of standard low-income housing.

Writing in late 1967, after civil disorders occurred in several urban renewal cities, Clive Entwistle made the following observations:

> Thus slum clearance is out of favor. It is true that much hardship has been caused by the particular way in which slum clearance has, in the main, been effected. Too few apartments at too high a rent have usually been provided for the substandard housing that they re-placed. It has generally been deficient in public facilities and com-munity structure, and environmental beauty has almost never been achieved. This has naturally and rightly resulted in a wave of politi-cal opposition by the dispossessed.
>
> The mistake, of course, was not one of principle, but of scale and method. It is necessary not only to provide sufficient new accomoda-tion of the right kind and at the right rents (whether by subsidy of costs or of rents) but to provide a sufficient surplus of such accommo-dation as to create a vacancy rate that, on a progressive scale, would permit future demolition without any hardship whatever.[1]

Cities that cleared land before securing redevelopers often got into a great deal of difficulty, ultimately becoming vulnerable to the demands of any prospective redeveloper with virtually any scheme, just to get the land developed. This snatched the new-found power to determine future land use and design right out of the poor planners' hands.

Local government typically aimed its urban redevelopment program first at the economic health of the city—by creating a dynamic, dramatic complex, usually in the downtown, that would replace obsolete develop-ment, encourage business leaders to believe in the city's potential, and spin off additional private investment in its vicinity. As a technique, redevelopment can be invaluable in spearheading the economic revitalization of a city, and it lets new development go to downtowns and other built-up areas where the infrastructure and transportation network already exist.

Redevelopment is also a vital technique for preventing development of open land. Every undeveloped site in a city is under continual pressure for development. Lot by lot, site by site, urban America is becoming developed. Since the development desired by the owner and developer often exceeds what zoning permits, the city is frequently in a position to prevent it. Unfortunately, however, the spectre of all those juicy revenues frequently governs.

Although open space is turned into buildings all too often, the reverse seldom occurs. Few developed urban sites are turned into public parks. Unlike buildings, parks traditionally cost, rather than generate revenues. What happens, then, to unwanted built-up sites? Typically, they are abandoned, with the buildings left standing to cave in or become vandalized in time. Even when buildings are demolished, which is not too often because of steep demolition costs, topsoil is not spread over the rubble, because topsoil, too, is costly. A city's existing burden of parks maintenance is usually considered heavy enough without adding to it. Parks need not be financial liabilities, however. Nonprofit organizations can be used to raise part of the purchase price, and nominal admission fees can be charged for parking, skating rinks, merry-go-rounds, and other easily controllable facilities. Oddly enough, less vandalism is said to occur in recreation areas for which a fee is charged than in those that are free. Nonetheless, the fact remains: developed urban sites are seldom turned into parks. The answer for cities, then, is to keep the urban open space that already exists.

The perpetual construction of new housing and shopping centers on virgin land—ignoring the mammoth investment in infrastructure oriented to urban districts—will ultimately lead, where it has not already, to ghost cities, amorphous settlements, and open space so rare that it can be seen only on excursions. Redevelopment is therefore the answer for the new construction market in much of urban America. Street patterns can be partially altered if need be. Old buildings can be rehabilitated. Old monuments can be enhanced. That is what a modern city should be: a well-designed and workable mixture, with open land preserved as an essential asset.

REDEVELOPMENT PRINCIPLES

The following principles are intended to indicate how redevelopment may be used to rescue a city or an urban area within it. There are of course numerous other important principles; these represent a sampling.

Urban Design

Planning of an urban area starts with an overall framework plan and ends with the form of a fence. Although virtually all components of a plan are important, competence at two extreme levels distinguishes the splendid plan from the ordinary one. Especially in improving existing communities, what makes the difference is a combination of a sound framework plan at the beginning, and intricately worked out details of urban design near the end, where the environment is designed at the scale of a group of rooms. After the major blocks of functions, uses, relationships, and systems are organized and located and the plan descends in scale, small details are designed that furnish and fill up spaces, soften the existence of utilitarian features like rubbish cans and parking lots, or provide the more rural qualities of townscape that most of us enjoy in our outdoor home environments. In the improvement of a depressed inner-city area, sensitive attention to urban design detailing can provide the extra measure of enhancement greatly needed.

New and Old Combined

Effective renewal of older urban areas, considerably or partially blighted, includes the conservation and rehabiliation of suitable older buildings, as well as modern forms of urban design and technology designed to harmonize with the existing architecture and infrastructure. However, the mere retention and building of row houses in an endless grid of similar blocks fails to enhance a century-old area in an imaginative and meaningful way. With respect to new construction: to rebuild parts of blocks built in the 1890s, for instance, in the form and dimensions of the 1890s, but without the population or density of the 1890s, without the nearby open space, the work-trips, the prices, the incomes, or the technology of the 1890s, is regressive in terms of benefits and costs to today's inhabitants. To counteract the negative realities of poverty or high population in such an area today, an input of new technology, urban design, and contemporary architecture, if well-considered and carefully detailed, can result in a renewed area that contains both the best of the old and the best of the new.

Effect of Aesthetics

Aesthetic elements within a community, or their lack, may well affect people profoundly in a multisensoral, sometimes unconscious, way—a way that is more than visual. Such elements can consist of scattered objects and places or of three-dimensional spaces of certain proportions, or they can relate to workability and order. Lack of educated appreciation may not alter the impact of environmental aesthetic elements, or their absence, even though in this case their impact may be unconsciously felt.

Nature and Cities

The return of elements of nature to cities is one of the most valuable and easy means of improving community appearance. Not the least of these is the out-of-doors itself—the air, the sky, daylight, sunshine, clouds, stars and moon, rain and snow. This requires large, openable window areas, with blinds for privacy, within all structures occupied for long spans of time each day—apartments, factories, offices, and schools. It means, where possible, a small private yard, terrace, or balcony for each dwelling unit, with balconies located so as not to darken living room areas. Trees, shrubs, grass, and vines can do much to make ordinary man-made environments colorful and pleasant. These should be liberally provided in public areas. On the grounds of multifamily housing, space should be made available for tenant gardeners to grow flowers, vegetables, and fruit. In areas other than large parks, paving can take the place of grass if it is combined with trees, flowers, or shrubbery in a designed manner.

The pleasures of water in the city are well known. Fountains, with their visual joys and cooling effects, should be made plentiful in areas that have no natural bodies of water within them.

Human Scale

The need for human scale in city development requires the avoidance of bigness in new construction—the oppression of monster masses, huge slabs, and Pentagon bulks. Small components, or complex irregularities of shape, even if more costly, are essential for human scale and aesthetic enjoyment. Even though our numbers are increasing and our cities distend, our species does not change. An individual person is still one relatively small unit, whose daily needs and pleasures must still be served at his or her level and scale.

Neighborhood Focus and Agora

Every urban neighborhood requires a central focus in physical form that provides the residents with the feeling of neighborhood identity, and it must be properly located and designed with one or more open plazas to afford a sense of place within it. In neighborhood improvement, where such focal points already exist, in whole or in part, they should be enhanced, and where they do not exist, they should be created. Elementary schools are the ideal main features of such neighborhood centers. Community facilities should be located within school buildings, where possible; convenience shops may be clustered close by.

Larger residential districts, consisting of groups of neighborhoods, should be identified by larger community centers, or agoras. Each agora should include community facilities, particularly those serving older children and adults, convenience and shopping retail outlets, cultural and amusement centers, and civic offices. Each agora must include a high school, college, or intermediate school, containing space for many of the community facilities, because of the agora's ability, by its size and normal activity, of generating urban liveliness.

Physio-Economic as Social

Improvement of the physical environment, particularly as it provides housing, schools, community facilities, industry, and transportation—in the right amounts, at the right prices, at the right locations, and of the right sizes and types—can be as important a function of social planning as effective social services or manpower training.

Staged Redevelopment

Intelligently staged redevelopment is as important as spatial and structural planning. Made especially difficult because of its incessant nature, it is both achievable and rewarding. Large-scale simultaneous demolition, without redevelopers under contract, is extremely risky for the city, hard to bear by relocatees, and an insult to other residents who feel adrift in a sea of vacant parcels for months or years on end.

Timing of Relocation

Effective timing of relocation, also difficult, can be achieved. It involves the timely acquisition of slums and the development of new housing to implement, ideally, the relocation of low-income families directly from blighted units into new low-income units.

Citizen Participation

Truly representative citizen participation can be accomplished. It is vital to good city and neighborhood planning. Enlightened citizens, often apathetic, are nevertheless imaginative and will support comprehensive, well-planned, and progressive programs. Their interest must be tapped and their involvement organized continually. It is, however, crucial to avoid letting special interest groups, raising false issues and crises, put the planning operation on a crisis-to-crisis basis, exploiting fear at every turn, and consuming valuable staff time.

Importance of Operational Techniques

The right kind of operation of some physical facilities is even more important than their existence. A needed bus route is merely a source of frustration if buses are infrequent and untimely, or if the fare is too high. A daycare center is useless to mindful parents if the staff is inadequate in terms of quality or quantity. Any good renewal plan will include operational standards, and its effectuation will include binding assurance that it will be carried out.

NATIONAL RENEWAL

Because of the civil disorders in urban renewal cities in the summer of 1967, urban renewal suddenly became anathema in many quarters. The National Commission on Civil Disorders subsequently ranked them as major, serious, and minor. Those in Chicago and Philadelphia were ranked as minor, in Boston and New Haven as serious, and in Detroit and Newark as major.[2] Although no shot was fired in New Haven's "riot," the city became stigmatized because of its heavy urban renewal involvement. An anchorman on NBC-TV's *Nightly News*, David Brinkley, related the federal money to New Haven's disorder and dismissed the entire renewal effort with one glib, pungent phrase. His statement ran somehting like this: "So, we have spent millions of dollars on New Haven—more per capita than on any other city. Obviously money is not the answer!" It was a shudderingly simplistic, almost fiendish, characterization.

I found it odd that it occurred to so few people at the time that the problem was that not enough money was spent in New Haven, where I was a renewal project director for six years until 1965. More money was needed in low-income neighborhoods for new public housing, remedial education, meaningful job training, drug and alcohol rehabilitation, day care, psychotherapy, social services for the mentally ill, additional moderate-income housing, equitable financing for homeowner rehabilitation, and the like. The job was far from complete in 1967. Social renewal was just getting started.

Urban renewal was a program that was forging the way, that needed to be broadened in scope rather than diminished, that needed to be corrected and amplified to make it fully workable on a national scale. (The Model Cities program was such an embryonic effort.) Instead, it was denounced and dismantled. It was gone by 1973.

Before urban America can be truly renewed, the nation has to change its priorities. Hypothetically, if one city improves and others do not, there is no way it can safeguard its new status, no way to prevent an overwhelming influx of needy people, pulling the city's finances to rock bottom again. Today improvement cannot be done city by city. Meaningful, lasting urban improvement can only be accomplished on a national scale with, for example, national economic planning, rich national educational programs, real economic safety nets for the unemployed, powerful national wars against racism, crime, drug traffic, and street gangs. National solutions have to be found for the errors of home rule, the demise of unskilled and semiskilled jobs, the high cost of construction, the sometimes-outlandish labor contracts, and inadequate health care—before the burden is shifted to cities or even states. Moreover, the nation's wealth has to be redistributed, turned back to sensible proportions. Oligarchical capitalism has to evolve into equitable capitalism before the country can expect any city, even with abundant aid, to be lastingly and thoroughly renewed.

NOTES

1. Clive Entwistle, "Total Habitat," p. 19.
2. The New York Times Company, *Report of the National Advisory Commission on Civil Disorders* (New York: Bantam Books, 1968), pp. 113, 158-59.

8

Housing

By far the largest land use in any city is housing, usually 70 to 90 percent, and a residential neighborhood can be beautiful, drab, or hell on earth. In my lifetime the hell-on-earth neighborhoods in urban America, frequently ghettos, seem to be on the increase and becoming more hellish, despite the existence of a city planning profession, despite scattered successful efforts.

THE HOUSING PROBLEM

Low- and moderate-income housing was a prominent issue of the late 1960s, partly because of the 1967 civil disorders. In almost twenty years the nation had not even met the new housing requirements expressed by Congress in 1949. From time to time in those days the federal government published staggering figures of new low-income housing units needed. Units supplied never came close—amounted, in fact, to a small fraction of those needed. For the most part, governmental assistance involved private development and it was not working, certainly not in terms of adequacy. As indicated in Chapter 2, only about 1.3 million units of low-income public housing were built nationwide between 1937 and 1985. Today the U.S. government does not even bother to broadcast the current housing need. The crisis figures are presented to us in human form, as we step over homeless people lying on our sidewalks. Our society is reduced to a new level of decay in which a significant portion of our poor and mentally ill live in the wild—the urban wild. Like deer, raccoon, and opossum, they huddle in the open air, trying to acquire the survival skills of a new breed of humanity.

An estimated 500,000 people are homeless in America (some estimates go as high as 3 million), of which perhaps 30 percent suffer from severe mental disorders.[1]

Almost a third of the nation (32 percent) is "shelter poor"—about 27 million households or 78 million people: after paying for their housing, "shelter poor" families do not have enough income left over for other necessities. And this does not even include the homeless![2]

Among sheltered households, many must pay over 50 percent of their income on housing and/or double up with other families to maintain shelter.[3]

Some of those paying less than 25 percent of their income on rent are also shelter poor—for example, families made up of three or more persons.[4]

Often welfare grants do not provide enough income to meet the cost of rental units available. "Fair market rent" in thirty-three states exceeds an entire welfare grant (Aid to Families with Dependent Children).[5]

A one-bedroom apartment is beyond the reach of at least one-third of rental households in every state. (About one-third of American households are renters.) In six states a one-bedroom unit is beyond the reach of over 50 percent of rental households.[6]

The slightest negative change in rental cost or income puts shelter poor families like these into the street.

This grave state of affairs is steadily on the increase. Not only have insufficient low-income units been constructed to meet the national need, millions of affordable apartments have been destroyed or taken out of the low-rent pool through arson, disinvestment by owners or lenders, or gentrification.[7] The number of families in dire circumstances grows continually. Figures provided here cover the period 1987 to 1990. Dozens of other staggering housing statistics reinforce this brutal story.

Meanwhile, the middle- and upper-income homeowners of America are given huge federal tax-deduction "subsidies" each year. In 1987 these housing subsidies amounted to almost $50 billion, nearly four times the federal housing funds directed to the poor and working class, many of whom were desperate.[8] A remarkable contrast.

This housing condition is an unspeakable outrage, yet it is a full-blown reality. It is the great disgrace of modern American life. Unbelievably, Congress does not seem to be alarmed. Even the Congressional liberals, occasionally promoting the solution of other domestic ills, fail to be alarmed about low-income housing. For example, in 1989 the Democratic Senatorial Campaign Committee sent me, as a registered Democrat presumably, a "Priorities Survey" listing ten critical issues to rank in order of importance. Housing was not even included, either by itself or as a conceivable part of another issue. Subsequent to my letter to Senator George

Mitchell, the chairman, complaining about this omission, I received another copy of the survey, and no answer from him. And in a revised survey received in July of 1992 housing was still omitted.[9] Do people today really have to be part of a huge voting block, similar to "The Elderly," for our representatives to take appropriate notice of their plight? Not long ago, "liberal" meant representing, among others, those unable adequately to represent themselves.

Already the homeless seem to have become an ethnic group—a people with a permanent, unshakable characteristic, like race or national origin, as if getting a decent house or apartment were out of the question for any of them, once homeless. This view is frighteningly underscored by media references to designing "better" or "permanent" homeless shelters. The homeless shelter must not become a new residential mode, alongside houses and apartments. The homeless shelter must be viewed as a temporarily necessary but repugnant phenomenon.

Adequate numbers of low- and moderate-income housing units would eliminate about 70 percent of homelessness, based on the 30 percent mentally-ill figure cited. Group homes with service centers for the mentally-ill homeless would eliminate much of the rest. The solutions are a bit more complicated than that, but these are the core components.

In June of 1991 a bookstore offered for sale a 123-page, spiffy little paperback by the National Alliance to End Homelessness entitled *What You Can Do to Help the Homeless*.[10] It was stacked up near the cash register, probably to persuade caring people to include it among their purchases. Only two pages of this book, as it turned out, are devoted to contacting one's senators and congressmembers to demand more federal fiscal assistance for housing. Four excellent pages are devoted to the prevention of homelessness, and seven paragraphs address federal housing cutbacks and the need to expand the supply of low-income housing. But these unsurpassingly important solutions are given eight pages out of 123, and they are mincingly placed among paragraphs calling for remedial volunteerism — help in soup kitchens, clothing drives, legal aid, and the like.

Even volunteering to help build low-cost homes, as is done by Habitat for Humanity, recommended in this book, provides an infinitesimal result when compared to the need. The need, says the book in a small paragraph on page 13, is for 5.5 million additional units of low-income housing. On another page we are told that Habitat has built 3,000 units thus far. That comes to 0.05 percent, or five one-hundredths of 1 percent, of the need. Moreover, it is by no means clear that 5.5 million units would even be anywhere near enough, with 27 million shelter poor households and half a million or more people homeless. It is essential that interested people grasp the magnitude of the housing problem, get a handle on the numbers, and stop advocating puny solutions.

The clarion call to arms that is necessary to get Congress effectively to address the tremendous need for low-income housing is not found in this disappointing book for popular consumption. Does this represent an inability on the part of the authors to grasp the magnitude of the problem, or is it a fear of facing an overwhelming social iussue that calls for "radical" solutions?

THE SOLUTION

Housing is a right, and it is more than a right. Housing is a necessity of life, along with food and clothing. It is monstrous to be obliged to do battle for this truth in a rich, democratic country.

Every American citizen must be guaranteed the availability of a workable dwelling that he or she can afford, through the expenditure of reasonable economic effort, located in a pleasant and well-organized environment.

The national government must be responsible for carrying out the housing construction it has intermittently called for since World War II.

Advocated here is a huge program of public housing, in amounts sufficient to house all low- and moderate-income Americans needing homes. Public housing is also proposed for middle-income families whenever the level of need is not met by private development. The proposal spreads out as follows:

City residents would be offered a "third choice" in urban housing types. Among residences in good condition within large metropolitan areas, the housing client has been, for most of this century, confined to two choices—the sterile brick, multi-storied construction of the city and the suburban-like house on the landscaped lot. A third choice is badly needed, one that combines the aesthetics and natural elements of the suburban house with the privacy, community, and interesting location of the urban apartment, plus the structural possibilities and excitement offered through a commanding use of modern technology. (See also "Nature and Cities," Chapter 7.)

In terms of apartment types, public housing for low-, moderate-, and middle-income would be the same—room sizes, closets, closet doors, kitchen and bathroom equipment, window area, soundproofing of walls, heights of ceilings, and so on. (From the point of view of apartment layout, the only relevant difference between low- and middle-income families today lies in family size and number of children. This difference can be handled through the design of large apartments that can be readily divided when and if small families become prevalent.)

Public housing would be part of planned neighborhoods, with new buildings imaginatively built alongside older structures, created to enhance the overall character of each neighborhood. (Scattered sites can mean isolated buildings in the urban hinterland.) Schools, parks, play areas, shopping, health facilities, recreational and cultural facilities, and attractive and functional transportation would be included in all neighborhoods, as well as cosmopolitan facilities such as outdoor cafes, pensions for young people starting adult life, meeting places of all kinds, and pleasant rooming houses and apartments for older people. Facilities would also be provided to house organizations attempting to bring about social change for the poor—functional manpower programs, remedial education, family counseling, and the like.

The financing of all this public housing would be in the category of direct building by government for low- and moderate-income housing. For middle-income households, financing would come from profit-free credit mechanisms. These might also be used for low- and moderate-income housing in some cases.

Homeownership has often been found important in terms of family well-being and good dwelling maintenance. Thus when incomes permit, tenants would be assisted in purchasing their units. To increase homeownership in Britain, publicly-built dwellings have been sold to their tenants (not to middle-income homebuyers); this has raised the number of owner-occupied homes from 50 percent in 1979 to 66 percent in 1987.[11]

Despite certain terrible examples of high-rise public housing, much already built around the country is in garden apartments. And eligible people like public housing, as evidenced by the extremely long waiting lists in most cities; often the number of people on waiting lists equals the total number of public housing apartments in existence.[12]

Public housing for armed forces personnel within the United States has come right out of direct allocations from Congress to the Defense budget. This has occurred where private off-base family housing was inadequate within the community. Indeed, as of 1988 the Department of Defense had built approximately 450,000 family housing units off-base for military personnel. Congressional appropriations to the Defense budget were also used for maintenance and modernization.[13] Let the naysayers take note. This is public housing for American moderate- and middle-income families, and it is built and financed by the government *because it is needed.* That is the very thing being proposed in this chapter.

Housing has been treated as a necessity of life in several European democracies and Israel for some time. Moreover, the record of low-rent housing construction in these and other democratic countries has proven that direct building and nonprofit financing by government are the answer.

After World War II the government of the Netherlands made sure its people were adequately housed. The record of public financial assistance

as a percentage of total national expenditure in Dutch housing in 1949
was as follows:[14]

State direct building	3.00
State subsidies	14.50
State loans	9.50
Municipal direct building	30.50
Municipal subsidies	.75
Municipal loans	17.50
Total Public Expenditure	75.75

Thus private financing in that year amounted to less than 25 percent.
Even today in some Dutch cities public funding of new urban housing
amounts to as much as 50 percent and is of high quality, according to
architect Richard Rogers. "Designed by the country's youngest, brightest
architects, it tends to be highly sensitive to its urban context and yet incor-
porates the spirit of innovation."[15]

Since independence, Israel has built thousands, perhaps millions, of
housing units through direct government building. Of the 70,000 new
units built by 1951, one-half were built by the government.[16] In 1972, 42
percent were built by the government.[17]

In Sweden 44 percent of the dwellings constructed in 1972 were built
through government enterprise, 39 percent in England and Wales, 64
percent in Northern Ireland (1970), and 80 percent in Scotland (1970).[18]
In that same year only 1.4 percent of new housing in the United States
was built by government enterprise. The remaining 98.6 percent was constructed with private financing.[19]

The HLM organizations in France (public housing authorities) are considered to bear a "social obligation" to provide low-cost housing, similar to
each council's obligation in British localities. As of 1983 the 1,100 HLMs
had built 2.8 million housing units in 37 years.[20] By contrast, the United
States, a nation more than four times the size of France in population,
had built only 1.3 million housing units in 48 years (1937-85). The HLMs
have been responsible for 30 percent of the housing built in France since
World War II. Some HLM units have gone to families who are not in the
greatest need, but this is offset by the fact that "social" housing is also built
by mixed economy companies—moderate-income housing renting at
below-market rates. The national government has much to say about
when and where HLM housing will be built. Construction is liberally
financed through low-interest, long-term national government loans (2-3
percent, forty years or more).[21]

The principal organization for mortgage loans to home buyers in

France is Crédit Foncier, a semi-public bank that provides loans guaranteed by the national government.[22] Terms are liberal. Other funds come largely from ingenious nonprofit and semi-public sources. In the early 1970s about 90 percent of all French housing was built with some form of governmental financial aid.[23]

Without considerable governmental assistance, housing built for profit cannot house low- and moderate-income famiies. These European governments take care of the housing needs of their lower-income people, and they do it without squandering tax funds on developer and lender profits.

Despite the infuriating bureaucratic practices and red tape that come to mind when one contemplates governmental operations, the U.S. government has proven it can do a superlative, efficient job when it tries—World War II, the Tennessee Valley Authority, the continuous excellent operation of overcrowded airports, and even the space program prior to 1986, including the trip to the moon.

In light of the prevailing attitude in this country toward liberal and social welfare causes, this public housing proposal may amount to a "wish list." Nevertheless, this is what I believe is needed, and I want no part in tinkering around with inadequate tax shelter programs and partnerships with banks and developers. The numbers would not come out right—the need would still outstrip supply by a mile—just as it has since 1960 or earlier. The financing of public housing has in the past been accomplished through the sale of tax-exempt bonds to private investors.[24] This can be done again.

On November 29, 1990, Congress signed into law the Cranston-Gonzalez National Affordable Housing Act after three years of wrangling. It is significant that the act covered two years, one of which, FY 1991, was immediately out of the picture because of the delay—HUD's appropriation for FY 1991 had already been enacted with different programs and funding levels. Funding for new public housing for FY 1992, unencumbered by special setasides, came to $553,600,000 nationwide, not even one billion dollars for new public housing in the United States of America.

NOTES

1. Anastasia Toufexis, "From the Asylum to Anarchy," *Time* (October 22, 1990), p. 58, and Nancy Gibbs, "Answers at Last," *Time* (December 17, 1990), p. 45.

2. Michael E. Stone, *One-Third of a Nation* (Washington, D.C.: Economic Policy Institute, 1990), p. 1.

3. Cushing N. Dolbeare, *Out of Reach* (Washington, D.C.: Low Income Housing Information Service, 1990).

4. Stone, *One-Third of a Nation*, p. 1.

5. Dolbeare, *Out of Reach*.

6. Ibid.

7. Working Group on Housing, *The Right to Housing* (Washington: Institute for Policy Studies, 1989), pp. 9, 14-15, and Dolbeare, *Out of Reach*.

8. Working Group on Housing, *The Right to Housing*, p. 18.

9. Democratic Senatorial Campaign Committee, "Democratic Senate Priorities Survey" (1989), and "1992 Priority Issues Survey" (Washington: 1989 and 1992).

10. Thomas L. Kenyon with Justine Blau, The National Alliance to End Homelessness, *What You Can Do to Help the Homeless* (New York: Simon & Schuster/Fireside, 1991).

11. David Brand, "All Revved Up," *Time* (June 22, 1987), p. 37.

12. Working Group on Housing, *The Right to Housing*, p. 20.

13. Ibid., p. 57.

14. United Nations Economic Commission for Europe, *Methods and Techniques of Financing Housing in Europe* (Geneva, Switzerland: 11 February 1952), p. 271.

15. Richard Rogers, "Capital Punishment," *Sunday Times Magazine* (London: March 1, 1992), p. 23.

16. Charles Abrams, ed. *Urban Land Problems and Policies* (New York: United Nations, Housing and Town and Country Planning, Bulletin 7, 1953), p. 87.

17. United Nations, Department of Economic and Social Affairs, *World Housing Survey, 1974* (New York: 1976), p. 174.

18. Ibid., pp. 174-76.

19. Ibid.

20. Ian Scargill, *Urban France* (New York: St. Martin's Press, 1983), p. 90.

21. Ibid., pp. 90-91.

22. Ibid., p. 89.

23. U.S. Department of Housing and Urban Development, Office of International Affairs, Urban Growth Policy Study Group, *Urban Growth Policies in Six European Countries*, a report presented to the Subcommittee on Housing of the Committee on Banking and Currency, House of Representatives (Washington: November 1, 1972), p. 57.

24. Working Group on Housing, *The Right to Housing*, p. 57.

9

Traffic and Transportation

New facilities and improvements for the movement of motor vehicles are by nature traffic-inducing. Developed to increase flow and convenience, they instead have disastrously increased usage. As long as the usage of expressways and major thoroughfares is unassigned as to who and how many may use them at any one time—as is the usage of theaters and airplanes for which seat-specific tickets are sold—widenings and improvements of major thoroughfares will encourage overutilization and unbearable traffic tieups. Yet governments keep on doing it, to this very day, at tremendous cost to everyone.

Transportation planning has to be part of general planning and kept in balance, public versus private, rail versus road. Everything is related in the complex system of an urban area. Innovations need to be studied and promoted, where feasible. The private automobile is not only a great polluter of air. In congested overabundance it is a destroyer of the quality of life of the urban wayside public (engine noise, honking, and air pollution), as well as of the traveler (deep frustration and fury).

Good city plans enhance the streets of our downtowns, and they promote urban transportation that is free flowing and on time, that will not harm the ears, eyes, and nervous systems of the wayside public, and that will be a delightful experience in and of itself.

Unfortunately, there are two kinds of people in the transportation world—rail people and motor vehicle people. The polarization is pronounced, and the motor vehicle people have won.

Until December 1987 it looked as if they had won for the following reasons:

(1) Because the only people interested in traffic and transportation

issues (with a few exceptions like this planner) were traffic engineers and transportation planners who had narrow priorities.

(2) Because traffic engineers had convinced authorities that trolleys and their tracks and waiting platforms obstructed the free flow of thoroughfares and that buses, by their flexibility within the roadbed, almost as flexible as cars, would afford a greater traffic volume.

(3) Because door-to-door shipping of cargo by trucks was more cost-effective than the old rail-plus-trucks system.

(4) Because railroad companies could not support unprofitable passenger service once their lucrative freight business was drastically reduced.

(5) Because the "rubber lobby" made up of companies that produce motor vehicles, tires, and gasoline, had successfully persuaded Congress that the Interstate Highway Program was the way to go for both passenger and cargo travel.

(6) Most of all, perhaps, because the human being could not resist owning and using an automobile if he could afford to buy it, insure it, and park it, even if near-perfect public transit was readily available.

After all, look at the new town of Vallingby in Sweden, whose planners minimized parking lots and garages and created superb rail service, only to discover that once a family could afford one, a car was purchased anyway for weekends and vacations.

And after all, look at the leading transportation expert of the mid-1960s who produced a textbook on traffic and transportation that contained not one word about mass transit. So secure was the motor-vehicular emphasis in those days that this expert apparently did not find it necessary even to give lip service to public transportation or rail travel. Spurred on by the general public's deep and enduring enthrallment with private car ownership, ease of parking, and unhindered forward motion while driving, the typical traffic engineer developed a regal self-image and disgracefully annulled the true needs of both the right-of-way travelers and the wayside inhabitants.

For a time it even looked as if the generalist planners could be blamed for the loss of trains and trolleys, at least in part. They had turned their backs on trolleys and railroads and on the whole question of urban traffic and transportation in the mid-1950s when the Federal Highway Trust Fund was being established. They still do to a large extent. Most allowed the traffic engineers to turn circulation into an arcane mystique, "too technical and complex for generalist planners to understand or cope with," and to turn many cities into places in which the storage and movement of motor vehicles were their most significant municipal functions. The typical generalist planner shrank from traffic and transportation planning as a lover of furry mammals shrinks from reptiles. Upon reflection, however, it became clear that blame directed at the massively overpowered planners carried with it the erroneous assumption that their involvement in the rail–motor fray would have made a difference.

For decades, therefore, it seemed that some of the sad-but-legal realities listed above were responsible for the loss of trolley cars and other rail services in the rail-versus-motor-vehicle fracas.

Then on December 6, 1987 the television news program "60 Minutes" widely exposed, for the first time as far as can be discerned, the criminal conspiracy that wrecked and annihilated the trolley car transit systems in forty-four American cities between 1936 and 1946.[1] The defendants were General Motors Corp., Standard Oil Company of California, Firestone Tire and Rubber Company, Mack Manufacturing Corp., Phillips Petroleum Company, and four other lesser-known companies, one of which, National City Lines, Inc., a holding company, was listed in legal records as the principal defendant. Various officers of the companies were also convicted. The plaintiff was the U.S. government, and the criminal conspiracy convictions were upheld on appeal.[2]

The illegal operating procedures were as follows: One or more of the more powerful corporations would finance the purchase of a city's existing trolley system by the holding company, National City Lines, Inc. Rails would begin to be pried up the next day, if possible. New General Motors buses, guzzling Standard Oil's fuel, riding on Firestone's tires, would make their appearance in the city shortly thereafter.

With a short headline identifying National City Lines as guilty in a trust case, the *New York Times* covered these March 12, 1949 convictions on March 13 of that year (Chicago, AP). The opening paragraph states that National City Lines, Inc. and fourteen other firms and individuals were convicted of antitrust charges by a jury consisting of twelve housewives, who considered their verdict for over thirty-six hours. The report continues that the crime of which all defendants were found guilty was that of conspiracy to monopolize commerce and trade in the purchasing of petroleum products, tubes, tires, and buses. It is not until the fifth paragraph out of a total of six that the report provides the names of the considerably more well-known defendant companies, and it is on page 79 of the main section of the Sunday edition that this news report may be found, along with the weather report and "Today's Index." (The news report in question was not listed in the index.)[3] All other articles covering this case in the *New York Times* from 1947-49 appear on the financial pages of previous weekday editions on pages 38, 40, 36, 39, 37, and 44. Headlines of these reports fail to draw the readers' attention to the scope of this conspiracy or the nationwide importance of the corporate defendants; only one secondary headline instructs readers that G.M. and Firestone are defendants.[4] With this kind of reportage, it is not surprising that potentially interested people were unaware all these years of this conspiracy and its transportation and urban planning implications in the forty-four affected cities across the country. Victims included Los Angeles, Baltimore, St. Louis, Oakland, Salt Lake City, Spokane, Mobile, Montgomery, Lincoln, San Francisco, and other cities in Florida, Iowa, Mississippi, Michigan, Texas, Ohio, California, and Illinois.

Washington, D.C. was not included, but the removal of its trolleys was probably an indirect result of this case. I remember in 1943-44 the wonderful, big "Presidential Trolleys," very streamlined, that glided through the streets of the capital with such near-silence and serenity, the same attractive, clean, and efficient cars that Philadelphia still uses on its Subway-Surface lines.

Penalties established by the court were ludicrous: $5,000 (maximum penalty) for each of the corporations and $1 for each of the individual executives. By 1955 trolley lines were gone from 90 percent of American cities. How overpowered can you get?

In place by 1920, LA's trolley lines carried over 200 million passengers by 1944, on over 1,000 miles of track, with 2,800 runs a day, often at one-and-a-half minute intervals. It was the biggest streetcar system in the country — hard to even imagine now that we know Los Angeles as a city afflicted with carbon monoxide and ozone air pollution primarily caused by its excessive automobile traffic on its extensive freeway system.

Early Los Angeles freeways met the volume on opening day that their traffic engineers had forecast for ten years hence. This was a failure to imagine the freeway as a motor car-inducer. Again, without selling reserved tickets, how can abundant numbers of people be averted from choosing to use the new expressway at any one time?

These days we find Los Angeles contrite. Its metropolitan region is turning itself inside out to return the region to livability with a draconian 1989 air quality plan calling for dozens of stringent measures including new public transportation and the elimination of gasoline-fueled cars within eighteen years — a plan somewhat watered down by September 1990.[5] (Incidentally, this plan was not triggered by planners but by a regional environmental agency. Nonetheless, its urban planning implications are vast and deep.) Needless to say, General Motors and the automobile industry are concerned about this turnabout to their fortunes.[6]

The new metro rail and trolley lines (sometimes called light rail lines) for Los Angeles are planned to run almost exactly where the old trolley lines were located long ago. But the right of way that carried trolleys down the middle of the Hollywood Freeway has been sold off; this means expensive new land purchases for new lines along this route. Los Angeles may yet regress to modern 1944 levels within this decade. What a century!

San Diego is on the move. Since 1981 the city has increasingly introduced new trolley routes. According to a statement by Mayor Maureen O'Connor in 1987, the trolley system has been very cost-effective and extremely popular with the public, especially for work trips. Mayor O'Connor has found that one section of San Diego would surely experience gridlock without the trolley and that trolleys are not only good for the city but cheap and fun, as well.[7] As of December 1987, nineteen other American cities were following in San Diego's footsteps. According to LA's mayor, Tom Bradley, car drivers will be obliged to adapt to a rapid transit system, because they really have no choice if they want to move. The first leg, the Blue Line, began running in July 1990.

It would be irresponsible not to mention the roughly 48,000 travelers killed in motor vehicle accidents each year and 5.5 million injured. The numbers for railway accidents amount to a tiny fraction of those involving motor vehicles.[8]

What happens to a city's transportation system has everything to do with the city's quality of life. Judges like the one who in 1949 fined the individual defendants $1 know that they, personally, can easily afford to move out of a city when its air quality becomes intolerable, leaving the have-nots and not-so-haves to live on in the unhealthy, depressing mess they left behind, thanks in part to their inequitable brand of justice.

Although we have Amtrak (for the moment), by and large, America sneers at public transport and at the people who depend on it. Somehow, for example, the Greyhound Bus Company was allowed to acquire the Trailways Bus Company, leaving the country with one major intercity system. Then this one company faced a drivers' strike. After an interminable number of years and months, too many small cities remain unserved by any intercity public transportation at all.

NOTES

1. CBS News, "60 Minutes," "Clang, Clang, Clang Went the Trolley!" Harry Reasoner, reporter, Patti Hassler, producer (New York: December 6, 1987), (Television program) Transcript pp. 10-13.

2. U.S. Courts—Abstracts of Cases:

    a. 68 S. Ct 1169 (1948).
       United States v. National City Lines, Inc., et al. United States Supreme Court. Decided April 18, 1948. (Issue of venue for the trial.)

    b. 186 F.2d 562 (1951).
       United States v. National City Lines, Inc., et al. U.S. Court of Appeals, Seventh Circuit. January 3, 1951. (The Court of Appeals upheld the 1949 convictions described in Chapter 9 herein. Because the 1949 trial was a jury trial, providing no judicial opinion, it was not abstracted in a federal digest.)

    c. 134 F. Supp. 350 (1955).
       United States of America v. National City Lines, Inc., et al. United States

District Court, N.D. Illinois. September 19, 1955. (Injunction sought to forestall future violations.)

3. "National City Lines Guilty in Trust Case." The *New York Times* (March 13, 1949), p. 79.

4. Gladwin Hill, "Transit Plot Laid to Nine Firms," The *New York Times* (April 11, 1947), p. 38.

5. Robert Reinhold, "Drastic Steps are Voted to Reduce Southern California Air Pollution," The *New York Times* (March 18, 1989), pp. 1, 8; Marla Cone, "Blueprint for Clear Skies," *Sierra* (July/August 1989), pp. 16, 18; Eric Mann, "LA's Smog Busters," *The Nation* (September 17, 1990), pp. front cover, 268-74.

6. Reinhold, "Drastic Steps," p. 8,

7. CBS News, "60 Minutes," pp. 12-13.

8. U.S. Department of Commerce, Bureau of the Census, *Statistical Abstract of the United States, 1990.* Tables 123, 1035, 1058.

10

European Planning Control

The inadequacy of city planning control in America is not related to its democratic form of government. Several constitutional democracies in Europe have serious and powerful city planning systems, notably Britain, France, and Sweden. Each system involves the national government, as well as various gradations of local authority. Sweden has used land banking to control patterns of urban growth, and all three countries exercise the powers of eminent domain and/or preemption. (Land banking enables the municipal government to purchase land well in advance of planned development and lease it to developers; preemption enables it to take the buyer's place, at the buyer's price, when a property is about to be sold.) Many other powerful means of implementation have been successfully used. Although procedures are complicated, especially in France and Britain, planning has dominion. Adequate funding is built into each system. Apparently these governments are ready and able to pay the price of sensible planning. Rational thought permeates these programs. Fairness and balance are paramount. The work of the city planner is legally sanctioned.

Regional planning operates in France out of a new fourth tier of government. Since 1982, when a major law was passed, France's territorial governmental units have consisted of national, regional (22 units), departmental (96 units), and commune (36,433 units), each administered by its own council elected by universal suffrage. The new law gave the lesser echelons greater power by providing that the deliberations of their councils no longer need be supervised by the prefects, consisting of departmental civil servants, nor subjected to preliminary checks by the national government.[1] Still, the prefects and an elite bureaucracy may well undertake technical planning, implemented through the enterprise of the relevant councils and the sponsorship of the central ministries.

France's strong tradition of urban planning is intricately bound up with private enterprise. With respect to the transformation of Paris in the 1960s, for instance, the various levels of government and the private sector worked together superbly in an effort to make the Ile-de-France a showcase of economic coordination and rational planning, according to H. V. Savitch. The master plan was a major tool: prepared by the regional prefect (even before the 1982 law), modified where necessary by the local authorities, and executed through the auspices of the central government. A 1960 master plan, PADOG, was a prominent force in the decentralization of factories from Paris. Similarly, the master plan of 1965, the *Schéma Directeur*, provided full-service destinations for Parisian industries relocating beyond the urban core. Savitch rejects any claim that "market forces" represented the primary or exclusive impetus for this Parisian transformation, because without government cooperating with the private sector, the transformation could not have occurred.[2]

International intelligence could not have proven more effective in avoiding interference by speculators:

> Work on the *Schéma Directeur* was carried out during the course of 1963 and 1964. It proceeded in some secrecy in order to avoid speculation in land at sites where proposals for development were being made and, in fact, maps with conflicting information were actually prepared in order to mislead those who were seeking to profit from the intentions contained in the plan.[3]

After permitting a few tall buildings to be built in Paris, notably the skyscraping Montparnasse Tower, Parisians began to regret this new departure in building height. As a result, the law was changed in the mid-1970s. Construction of skyscrapers was henceforth prohibited in Paris, to the relief and joy of lovers of Paris the world over. It was accomplished in part through a legal limit on density, the *Loi Galley*.[4] In addition, La Défense, just northwest of Paris, in the "first ring" of the Ile-de-France, was created as a compact community, emphasizing highrise office development. La Défense was built out of a widespread desire to retain the densities and relatively low skyline of Paris.[5]

> Unlike New Yorkers, Parisians believe in the efficacy and worthiness of "a plan." Planning is something the French do in order to plot their future and determine their priorities. Its carryover into state and local government is an integral part of the culture.[6]

In France planners are not normally obliged to do battle with private interests on development matters, as they are in American cities. Instead, as respected technocrats, planners are among the political elite—composed also of top elected officials and ministers—who are usually the sole negotiators of planning and development issues.[7] "Private enterprise has had to deal with a strong, insulated, and centralized bureaucracy. It is not uncommon for French developers to behave as supplicants to a powerful class of technocrats."[8] Jurisdictions that do not have planning agencies are provided plan preparation and development services by a central super-ministry, the DDE (*Direction Départmentale de L'Equipment*), which is decentralized with departmental field offices. The DDE supervises all environmental, planning, housing, infrastructure, and highway activities and functions within the state.[9]

> The local plan (POS) enshrines development rights for developers, with adherence to its provisions ensuring an authorisation for development. However, an approved POS is a prerequisite for the devolution of planning to the local level, and in its absence all development outside built-up areas is effectively prohibited, leaving the remainder of the country under the control of national regulations.[10]

Through French administrative law discretion is granted not to elected officials, as it is in the United States, but to administrators. Thus the DDE is fully empowered as the principal source of planning expertise, a situation further emphasized by the degree and complexity of planning control. This assures reliance by the numerous small communes on the DDE's skilled staff, and it dramatizes to local elected officials the need to gain proficiency in the intricacies of the *Code de L'Urbanisme* in order to play a significant role in the planning process.[11]

In the field planning control begins with a building permit requirement (*permis de construire*), which combines both planning and building control, and it has an enforcement procedure calling for the mandatory declaration of construction start, followed by potential strict inspections that can result in the stoppage of work if the construction deviates from permitted plans. A declaration must also be signed at the completion of work, with the architect or developer certifying to the building's conformity to the building permit. Random checks by technical inspectors may follow the issuance of a certificate of conformity, and if infractions are detected at this point, forceful sanctions, including demolition, may be established. But truly effective control, according to John V. Punter, lies in the inspections carried out by insurers or potential purchasers of the property and in the civil law liability held by the developer or architect if the *permis de construire* is not followed. Approximately 20 percent of certificates of conformity are initially withheld, amounting to 10 percent in the long run, establishing unimpeachable proof that the French enforcement system works exceedingly well.[12]

Development control in France has a built-in enforcement system to ensure conformity to planning provisions. The administrative courts provide an appeal system and an opportunity for legal redress for all actors in the process—including applicants, local authorities, affected individuals and environmental groups. Finally, despite decentralisation, the French State keeps a significant control over planning practice through the law, which prescribes the format of the POS and the procedure of decision-making, and through the state services (i.e., the DDE), which continue to exercise technical control in smaller communes.[13]

Savitch has a surprising observation about citizen reaction to planning in Paris and in France as a whole:

The lack of a forceful citizen opposition may seem curious for a nation that heralded the great revolutions of the modern age. It is doubly odd for the Ville de Paris, whose streets have been barricaded many times over. The paucity of mass protest may have more to do with the unique qualities of the subject matter than with the general nature of French politics. That is, decisions about the built environment have a different meaning to Parisians than do conflicts about religion, schools, wages, or foreign policy. The remaking of the built environment is more often perceived as a technical rather than a political issue. The French press treats decisions about the built environment under the less controversial captions of "urbanisme," "architecture," or "territorial development" rather than as a subject of political intrigue. Hence, the political consequences of redevelopment are not as consciously apprehended as they are in New York or London. Deference is more readily given to technocrats and planners, who are perceived to have the "correct solutions."[14]

After his immersion in Parisian city planning for a week or two in 1978, Edward J. Logue was impressed with French planning as compared to American. He speaks with enthusiasm about a French professional who treats city planning "as an essential discipline for policy analysis and implementation." He admires the "thorough and systematic approach" of these French planners.[15]

Although not all of the American group would endorse everything we saw and heard, there is no question that we found ourselves exposed to a program and city administrative arrangement which was clear about its values, its priorities, its resources, and its powers.[16]

In a 1992 article describing "How Paris Works," journalist Steven Greenhouse, who spent five recent years in Paris, maintains that despite some negatives like traffic congestion, growth in crime, and scarcity of affordable housing within the central city, by and large Paris is as "magical" and "transcendent" as we think it is. Public schools and day-care centers are excellent, parks are lush and beautiful, streets are swept and garbage collected every day, and cultural places and events are fostered and enhanced.

A controlling difference between Paris and New York appears to be the extent of state aid. The government of France pays 50 percent of most of Paris's capital projects, like sewers and schools, and 40 percent of the city's operating budget, according to Greenhouse. *In addition*, it pays most welfare costs, finances public hospitals, and pays the full salaries of the city's teachers, police, and firefighters.[17] The City of New York received about 4 percent of its fiscal 1991 capital budget from the New York State and U.S. governments combined, as well as about 34 percent of its operating budget for the same year.[18] Other cities share in France's urban success story. Lyon, Nice, Strasbourg, Bordeaux, and Toulouse have worked hard to maintain their beautiful, cultural, and vital cities that are attractive also to families. Greenhouse cites the declaration of Leo van den Berg, director of the European Institute for Comparative Urban Research at the University of Rotterdam, that a generous and concerned fiscal approach to cities is common to almost every nation in Europe.[19]

Planning control is remarkably powerful in Sweden:

> Post-war urban development in Sweden, internationally renowned for its successful solution of urban housing shortage and environmental problems, has been based on the twin pillars of a national urban policy made up of a building code and equitable tax and loan system which has enabled the central government to direct the type, extent and location of development, and a municipal planning enjoying extensive powers over land use and the production and distribution of a wide variety of technical and social services.[20]

Sweden is a parliamentary democracy that has had a socialist government since 1932, except for the six years starting in 1976 and except for a period starting in September 1991 when, probably owing to the worldwide recession, a group of nonsocialist parties gained a majority and formed a coalition.[21] Thus the national government was socialist for over sixty years (the Social Democratic Party is still the largest), and for most of those years the nation experienced almost ideal domestic prosperity. In 1971, for instance, Sweden had the second highest standard of living on earth.[22]

There are about 100 central administrative agencies in Sweden that, accompanied by the county administrations, enforce the laws. Each of the 24 counties and 286 municipal districts is headed by a council elected by universal suffrage that has the power to levy income taxes. Land use planning is the responsibility of both the national government and the municipalities under the 1947 Building and Planning Act and succeeding legislation. Municipal plans are ratified by county authorities who act as representatives of the national government, ensuring compliance with central planning policies and standards.[23] L. S. Bourne maintains that although municipalities and counties have a fairly exclusive lock on planning and development decisions, they still compete with each other for job- and tax-producing industries in the tradition of North America. Unlike its urban planning and social programs, Sweden's free-market economy has been largely unregulated, dominated by large domestic corporations and continental-market competition.[24]

Despite the virtual elimination of private land-use decisions within a municipality's plan area through land banking, preemptive purchase, or eminent domain, speculation in land and pressure from private owners and builders must constantly be dealt with, according to Abdul Khakee.[25]

Stockholm's aggressive land-acquisition program began in the early 1900s when a conservative municipal government started acquiring huge holdings outside the city limits. The following is from a 1972 account:

> All municipally-owned land is leased. Stockholm develops land in accordance with its plans rather than as a reflection of the market value of a given site. Land acquisition costs are aggregated so that the rents from a particular site need not return its acquisition cost to the city.[26]

By the early 1970s three-quarters of Stockholm's post-1945 housing had been constructed on municipally-owned land. Today each satellite community created outside Stockholm is served by a new subway rail line connecting it to the central city. Architects and planners have created a sense of place and neighborhood within each satellite center—through easy and safe pedestrian access to community facilities, schools, and shops, through separation of each center from the rest, and by creating a uniqueness in the character and design of each suburb.[27] After the mid-1970s new satellite centers were designed with greater architectural flexibility and variety than had been the case in the earlier international-school plans. By 1985 fourteen new suburban centers had been built north of Stockholm alone.[28]

Urban planning in Sweden is clearly dominated by planners. Perhaps out of a reluctance to make early commitments or to expose their ignorance, municipal politicians tend to accept the decisions of local planners. "It is planners who discuss and analyze alternative solutions." By and large, politicians limit their attention to final proposals.[29]

As of October 1991, the new Swedish coalition government planned to revitalize the national economy through tax reduction and other measures, but significantly, "social welfare will continue to be financed primarily by public means," official sources state.[30]

Modern British town planning started with the Town and Country Planning Act of 1947, which applied to the whole country and inextricably combined national planning policy with urban development, control of land values, and regulatory powers.[31] Britain's central government began at this time the development of thirty-two now-famous new towns, bypassing locally elected councils with centrally-designated development corporations.[32] The authority and responsibility of the national government prevail in British planning, even though planning of existing communities is undertaken by local, district, or county authorities.

Concerns about land use formed the basis of the new system of planning under the 1947 act: urban sprawl, congestion, mixing of land uses in the old sections, ribbon development along major collector roads, and the inevitable loss of agricultural land. Perhaps more important was the high unemployment in depressed regions, propelling migration to London and other large cities. According to H.W.E. Davies, however, land use problems provided the principal impetus for Britain's powerful new system of development control.[33]

Policies and strategies for regulating urban development in Britain have involved three major thrusts, according to Bourne: (1) attempting to limit the sprawl of cities through land use controls, such as conservation policies, planning permissions, and greenbelts, at the same time that some urban populations are relocated to new or expanded towns; (2) attempting to limit the creation of office or industrial jobs within congested urban areas, directing them to economically depressed areas through financial and employment incentives and governmental decentralization policies; and (3) controlling urban redevelopment through the limitation of private incentives not tied in with government-sponsored slum clearance and renewal efforts.[34]

Through Britain's 1947 act a comprehensive and compulsory planning system was established that identified the categories of development eligible for the new type of controlled planning, gave elected local councils the authority to approve applications for planning permission to use or develop land in a specific way, and made it their duty to undertake land use and development plans for their jurisdictions. England's minister of town and country planning, later the secretary of state for the environment, was given the duty and authority to oversee local planning—approve plans, hear appeals, and intervene, where necessary—making decisions on applications for planning permission or taking responsibility for land use and development plans.[35] The Department of the Environment is also responsible for England's housing, environmental protection, and countryside policy. (Wales, Scotland, and Northern

Ireland have similar central environmental departments with slightly different procedures.)[36] Unfortunately, the Local Government Act of 1985
abolished the Greater London Council and England's six metropolitan
county councils, effectively eliminating regional planning and making
coordinated land use planning extremely difficult, according to Richard
Rogers.[37] The various borough, district, and county authorities remain
responsible for local plans and development control. A 1990 government
pamphlet states that borough and district councils within London and the
metropolitan areas "are preparing new unitary development plans."[38]
Despite this perhaps temporary elimination of regional planning, planning control still prevails in England, with the secretary of state for the
environment providing powerful national oversight.

Thus for forty-five years town and country planning has been one of
Britain's finest jewels in the crown. Patsy Healey provides a compelling
observation concerning the prominence of landscape in British planning:

> The lifestyle of the landed class of the eighteenth century echoed
> through cultural middle class life in the nineteenth, and still sustains
> an imagery of country life and landscape which has a strong hold on
> British values. Environmental concerns in Britain thus have a his-
> tory which long precedes the contemporary international environ-
> mental movement. It is these values which gave momentum to the
> idea of planning both "town and country" in the 1940s, which
> underpinned the alluring image of the "garden city," which sustain
> strong policies for landscape protection (as in "green belts," "areas of
> outstanding natural beauty," "areas of high landscape value"), and
> which provide the cultural context for "containing" urban growth.
> The effectiveness with which these policies of landscape protection
> have been implemented is possibly the greatest achievement of the
> post-war planning system in Britain, and certainly one which strikes
> many visitors to this country accustomed to a less regulated ap-
> proach to landscape change.[39]

Davies observes that although control is a vital part of planning in
England, much greater attention has been directed, at least within professional circles, to the plans themselves:

> During the 40 years since 1947, when plans were being prepared,
> approved and revised through a very lengthy process; when the form
> and content of development plans was altered after exhaustive en-
> quiries and new legislation; when regional plans came and went;
> when new, non-statutory forms of policy guidance were first
> encouraged and then discouraged; during this entire period, devel-
> opment control has continued dealing with between 400,000 and

500,000 applications annually. The courts have also kept the definition of development under constant review during this time, firmly confining it to the use and development of land, despite attempts at widening the scope of plans. The government has periodically redefined the scope of permitted development. Management studies have been undertaken into control procedures, in an attempt to reduce delay. But, throughout this period, there has been virtually no challenge to the relationship between policy, represented by plans, and control.[40]

British planning became somewhat more market-oriented under Margaret Thatcher, prime minister from 1979 to 1990. A case in point is the London Docklands Development Corporation, a public development corporation designed to encourge bold, rapid private development in the huge Docklands redevelopment area, overwhelming the normal planning activities of the three boroughs it comprises. Normal restrictions and taxation for new businesses have been waived. Much has been built, most of it very pricey, including giant office towers. The Docklands development is not universally admired by any means and may well be an isolated blip in an otherwise powerful national planning system. Gradual reversion to pre-Thatcher planning control could eventually follow the 1992 bankruptcy of Olympia and York, developer of the unfinished, and pivotal, Canary Wharf office development in the Docklands area.[41]

Complaints about these strong planning systems exist, of course. Most prominent have been lack of flexibility, autocratic architects, and inadequate citizen participation. Developers ipso facto grouse about red tape, delays, and restrictions to their absolute freedom. By and large, however, these legally-controlled planning systems are admired and supported.

Other democratic countries in Europe have strong systems of planning control, as well. In Denmark, for instance, the national government provides a framework plan for the counties, which in turn provide framework plans for local government planning. Although of late the trend has been for a modicum of flexibilty, plans are used as legally-binding controls, and they have been strengthened with respect to protection of the natural environment.[42] Another example is the Netherlands. Dutch municipalities also have legally-binding plans, developed out of the context of national and regional framework plans. The Netherlands has, in fact, been called "the most planned country in Europe."[43]

When errors are revealed in the city planning systems of these European democracies, rational adjustments are made. The entire legalized procedure is not scuttled in favor of "privatization." Moreover, mistakes may be classified as errors in judgment, rather than as the spoils of the marketplace.

Of course there are program errors, and of course there are political changes. Nevertheless, it is fair to say this: Even if each of these planning control systems had been abolished after, say, twenty years by tidal waves of irrational politics, the message in the context of this work would be identical: it has been done in other democracies; it can be done in the United States. The urban planning profession has been a vital part of each country's land use and development control system. It could become a vital part of such a system in the United States.

Are these successes a function of size? The United States is far larger in population than any European country (249.6 million). The closest is Germany (79.1 million) with about a third of America's population. The population of the United States is over four times that of either Britain or France. Do these proportions mean that America is too huge and unruly to set up a similar system, working logically through the states, regions, counties, and municipalities? If that were true, it would also follow that Britain and France with 57.1 and 56.2 million people, respectively, would be too huge and unruly to be able to do what Sweden has done, because the population of each is over six-and-a-half times that of Sweden, with 8.6 million people. The point is they have, despite an even greater disparity in size than that between the United States and Britain or France.[44] Thus size is not a major factor in this difference in city planning systems. The major factor appears to be desire for rational governmental control versus the desire for maximum laissez-faire in land use and developmental policies.

What matters in the context of this work is the impact of these systems on urban life and development. The evidence is conclusive that in Britain, France, and Sweden it would be unthinkable for a private developer to initiate an outlying shopping center capable of ruining a nearby downtown by simply buying the land and applying for a local building permit.

Similarly, in these countries it would be well-nigh impossible for a national government mortgage program to inadvertently (or otherwise) dictate a deleterious human settlement policy, such as our post–World War II VA mortgage program, and permit it to effect significant repercussions for decades.

In these democracies such proposals are carefully measured against ongoing national, regional, county, and local urban policies—for the good of the commonweal.

NOTES

1. Ministry of City Planning and Housing, French Republic and the United Nations Economic Commission for Europe, Committee on Housing, Construction and Planning, *Human Habitation in France: Situation, Tendencies and Policies* (New York: June 1982), p. 14.

2. H. V. Savitch, *Post-Industrial Cities* (Princeton: Princeton University Press, 1988), pp. 128-29.

3. Ian Scargill, *Urban France*, p. 149.

4. Ibid., pp. 107-8.

5. Savitch, *Post-Industrial Cities*, pp. 126, 161.

6. Ibid., p. 159.

7. Ibid., p. 136.

8. Ibid., p. 134.

9. John V. Punter, "Planning Control in France," *Town Planning Review* (Liverpool, England: April 1988), p. 161.

10. Ibid., p. 179.

11. Ibid., p. 171.

12. Ibid., pp. 160, 167.

13. Ibid., p. 179.

14. Savitch, *Post-Industrial Cities*, p. 137.

15. Edward J. Logue, "Introduction," *Survival Strategies, Paris and New York*, ed. George G. Wynne (New Brunswick, N.J.: Transaction Books, 1979), pp. 10, 16.

16. Ibid., p. 10.

17. Steven Greenhouse, "Why Paris Works," the *New York Times Magazine* (July 19, 1992), pp. 16, 17, 24, 29.

18. Percentages derived from data provided in: City of New York, Elizabeth Holtzman, Comptroller, *Comprehensive Annual Financial Report of the Comptroller for the Fiscal Year Ended June 30, 1991*, pp. 53, 54, 130, 144; courtesy of the Citizens Budget Commission. *N.B.* Over 80 percent of the capital budget was financed by proceeds from the sale of bonds.

19. Greenhouse, "Why Paris Works," pp. 16, 24.

20. Abdul Khakee, "From Master Planning to Structural Planning," *Cities* (Oxford, England: November 1985), p. 318.

21. Swedish Information Service, *Fact Sheets on Sweden* (Stockholm: October 1991).

22. U.S. Department of Housing and Urban Development, Office of International Affairs, *HUD International, Information Series 20*, January 15, 1973, p. 1.

23. Khakee, "From Master Planning," p. 319.

24. L. S. Bourne, *Urban Systems: Strategies for Regulation* (Oxford, England: Clarendon Press, 1975), p. 120.

25. Khakee, "From Master Planning," pp. 325-26.

26. U.S. Department of Housing and Urban Development, *Urban Growth Policies in Six European Countries*, p. 57.

27. Ibid.

28. Eva Rudberg, *Stockholm 1920-1985* (Stockholm: Swedish Museum of Architecture, Summer Exhibition, 1985), pp. 2-4.

29. Khakee, "From Master Planning," p. 328.

30. Swedish Information Service, *Swedish News* (Stockholm: September 19, 1991 and October 4, 1991).

31. Patsy Healey, "The British Planning System and Managing the Urban Environment," *Town Planning Review* (Liverpool, England: October 1988), p. 403.

32. Luther A. Allen, "British and French New Town Programs," *Comparative Social Research*, ed. Richard F. Tomasson (Greenwich, Conn.: 1982), p. 276.

33. H.W.E. Davies, "Development Control in England," *Town Planning Review* (Liverpool, England: April 1988), p. 128.

34. Bourne, *Urban Systems*, p. 92.

35. Davies, "Development Control in England," pp. 127-28.

36. U.K. Foreign and Commonwealth Office, *Planning, Urban Regeneration and Housing in Britain* (London: August/September 1990), p. 1; U.K. Foreign and Commonwealth Office, *Local Government in Britain* (London: April 1991), p. 4.

37. Richard Rogers, "Capital Punishment," p. 23.

38. U.K. Foreign and Commonwealth Office, *Planning, Urban Regeneration*, p. 1.

39. Healey, "The British Planning System," pp. 400-401.

40. Davies, "Development Control in England," p. 135.

41. Savitch, *Post-Industrial Cities*, p. 227, and *New York Times*, May 28, 1992, pp. A1, D2.

42. D. Edwards, "The Planning System and the Control of Development in Denmark," *Town Planning Review* (Liverpool, England: April 1988), pp. 137-58.

43. H.W.E. Davies, "The Control of Development in the Netherlands," *Town Planning Review* (Liverpool, England: April 1988), pp. 207-25.

44. Mark S. Hoffman, ed., *The World Almanac and Book of Facts 1992* (New York: Pharos Books, 1991). U.S. population from 1990 U.S. Census final count of December 1991, p. 43. Populations of Britain (U.K.), France, Sweden: 1990 estimates, pp. 759, 804, 812. Population of Germany: 1991 estimate, p. 761.

11

Conclusion

Some of the urban problems that industrial and business decentralization has brought about are touched on in Chapter 1 — ghetto adolescents desperately needing work while jobs go begging in the suburbs unless employers extend special private transportation, unbearable rush-hour traffic congestion on suburban roads, huge megasuburbs and megacounties ("edge cities") that meet some needs of middle- and upper-middle-income families but have no ethnic or economic diversity, no downtowns, no sense of place, no spirit of community.

Middle-class suburban outflux figures are more frightening than ever, with the well-paid 35-44 age group moving to the suburbs as fast as it can, leaving central cities with even greater proportions of poor people, resulting in reduced tax revenues because of the cities' fiscal isolation from their suburbs. The suburbs should, of course, pay for some of the services for the central city's poor, but in most of the country home rule and municipal incorporation prevent the kind of annexation of unincorporated land that cities are permitted in a few sections, for example, in the West and Southwest. Except through higher-governmental aid, suburban towns are not going to share the city's burden in any significant way if not required to do so.

As more and more middle- and upper-income Americans live outside cities, the proportion of people *interested* in cities is severely curtailed, producing a critical lessening of concern in Washington. Indeed, the drastic reduction in federal aid to cities in the 1980s undoubtedly precipitated the urban impoverishment of the early 1990s, with some cities perhaps within a year or two of bankruptcy.

A few cities, such as those in the Southwest, are thriving today, while others approach third-world conditions. Urban violent crime with fire-arms has gone beyond the pale, including the wanton slaughter of children in their beds. Drug addiction, drug dealing, and the proliferation of vicious gangs are rampant and on the rise. Urban schools continue to be a disgrace. In Newark, New Jersey, the car-theft capital of the nation, inner-city youths admittedly steal cars for the thrill of it and for pride in the execution of a master skill, not simply for the money. The mayhem created is often deadly.[1] Increasingly, American cities are seen as breeders of decadence.

European democracies foster their cities as centers of culture, ideas, and creativity. The greatest democracy in the world, however, virtually turns its back on its own cities. Consider the aid-to-cities bill that took three years to get through Congress and was finally passed on November 28, 1990, the Cranston-Gonzalez National Affordable Housing Act, which, as we have seen, could apply only to Fiscal 1992. For that year $3.272 billion was authorized for community development. This amount divided by the nation's population comes to $13 per capita, as compared to $746 per capita spent by the federal government on urban renewal in 1965 in New Haven, Connecticut, and $277 per capita in Newark, New Jersey, just to give the reader a rough idea of where we are.[2] There will thus be little federal help for any city wanting to clear blighted urban land for redevelopment or fiscally assist in economic development. Considering the size of the problem, this is sheer tokenism.

In the summer of 1992, near press time, Congress was at it again. Undoubtedly in response to the April riots in South Central Los Angeles and the upcoming presidential election, the House of Representatives passed an "urban aid package" calling for $5 billion over six years for twenty-five urban enterprise zones and twenty-five "rural development zones"—again, money spread too thin for the sake of handing out slices of pork to places not desperately needing federal aid. Then the Senate Finance Committee produced a bill originally intended to respond to the Los Angeles riots but which in the end was a tax grab bag, with perhaps only a fourth of the funds aimed at urban ghettos.[3] More tokenism. These pieces of legislation came six months after the U.S. Conference of Mayors had requested a $34.8 billion federal package to aid the nation's cities: $15 billion in direct aid to cities based on degree of distress and unemployment, $5 billion for public works, $6 billion for community development, $4 billion for transportation, $2.8 billion for job training, $2 billion for small business loans.[4]

Given the character of our society today, it is not surprising that some of our cities are close to bankruptcy, receiving virtually no help from Washington. Our largely materialistic, consumer-oriented society discourages concern for moral values, especially since the service-be-damned, lucrative-only, bottom-line-ism inflicted on us by leading business schools in the 1970s. Preoccupation with selfish interests has taken full precedence over responsibility to the community.

In June of 1991, while NASA tried to inveigle $30 to $40 billion out of Congress for space station Freedom, NASA's chief made the amazing statement: "If we spent the space station dollars directly on education or housing or whatever, it still wouldn't cure the problems of cities or schools."[5] Then in July of that year a Senate subcommittee found a few billion dollars for the space station in part by cutting proposed funds for elderly housing. This followed a similar move by the full House of Representatives, which had cut public housing funds for this purpose. There is more. Senator Barbara Mikulski of Maryland, "whose state would be a large recipient of space station funding," claimed that the government was obliged to "retain America's preeminence through the space station,"[6] even though NASA's unnecessary launches into space may do enormous permanent damage to the earth's ozone layer,[7] and even though many scientists question the relative utility of the station. Much as I respect Senator Mikulski as a liberal Democrat, this illustrates admirably how vital national affairs can be subverted in favor of a constituent jobs program—this one to be financed solely by U.S. taxpayers. There is considerable evidence that NASA is without a clear mission, that it drains scarce money from more useful scientific projects, as well as from the kind of social, economic, and technological programs discussed in this work. The tail continues to wag the dog, with projects undertaken not for their essential value but primarily for the jobs they create, projects most certainly identifiable as "prosperity projects,"—those properly promoted only after the basic needs of the people are met, after the federal budget is balanced, and when the nation is in a true period of prosperity again.

This is the America that cares more for exploration in outer space than for meeting her people's ordinary needs. This is the America in which the wealthiest 10 percent of households controls approximately 68 percent of the nation's wealth (1983)[8]—Hamilton's oligarchical capitalism achieved to the fullest. This is the America that has an inexcusably high rate of illiteracy, an estimated one in every five adults, that ranks 49th in literacy out of the 156 United Nations member nations.[9] This is the America that in 1991 had a rate of incarceration of 426 persons per 100,000, as compared to South Africa's figure of 333 and the USSR's figure of 268,[10] whose median family income in 1991 had not increased since 1973 and whose average production-worker income had not increased since 1960.[11] This is the America that between 1975 and 1985 endured the impacts of an estimated two-thirds of its Fortune 500 companies convicted of serious crimes.[12] And this is the America whose racism caused a young black South African to be deeply shocked by what he found here—many towns divided into a white world and a black world. Mark Matha Bane, author of *Kaffir Boy in America*, protests that he did not escape apartheid's bondage only to find himself segregated in America. He further observes, referring to American ghettos: "I see we are dying in many of those places. Young people are growing up in homes where family life is unknown. For me, in South Africa, family was the citadel, the center that kept me alive." Bane decries the values that American society encourages for its young people to emulate. In real life and on television, he contends, this society glorifies materialism, villainy, cheating, and lying to achieve success.[13]

Speaking of the decades 1970-90 Archibald Cox states in a 1990 article:

> While the greed and luxury of the very rich became the stuff of popular culture, the number of homeless Americans swelled, as did the armies of hopeless youths who, denied the prospect of useful lives, turned to violence, drugs and crime. The infrastructure disintegrates. The promise of racial equality is frustrated partly by indifference and the return of prejudice, partly by economic disparities. Public education declines. The illusion of easy success born of the conquest of a continent and American might in two wars is punctured by foreign industrial competition. We are now a debtor nation.
>
> Not only do problems go unsolved but political leaders seem, for the most part, to make no effort to solve them. The S & L catastrophe is the result of default in political responsibility, as is the unwillingness to face up to the crushing national debt put upon future generations. The all-consuming inquiry—how do I get reelected—all too often becomes, how do I raise even larger campaign contributions from lobbyists, not how do we solve the problem for the public good.[14]

As John Kenneth Galbraith points out in his 1992 book *The Culture of Contentment*, these conditions are rooted in the fact that the Americans who vote in national elections are, by and large, supremely contented with their lot. With respect to the critical problems of the have-nots, this contented majority favors inaction by Congress, for example, no rise in taxes. The poor, in turn, tend to ignore elections, forfeiting their right to vote. Political incumbents and candidates recognize this alignment and identify "needs" accordingly, Republicans mainly for the upper-income groups, Democrats mainly for the middle, leaving the have-nots represented by that portion of the contented majority concerned with society's less fortunate—the liberals. Because of their limited number, liberals fail repeatedly to persuade the government to undertake an attack on the recession and institute other critically needed measures, including the renewal of inner cities. Understandably, members of the contented majority are happy with government "subsidies" for their own kind— income tax deductions of mortgage interest and real estate taxes for homeowners (see Chapter 8), federal insurance of bank deposits, farm-income supports, Social Security, and even the military. By contrast, Aid to Families with Dependent Children and other safey-net programs for people with no income are, in their view, ripe for reduction and reform.

But for the substantial voting support of the contented majority, Galbraith contends, government would have taken action by 1990 to get our national house in order through such measures as raising taxes on upper income brackets, moving substantial resources from the military to the support of central cities and states, and employing people in public works programs to rebuild infrastructure.[15]

> The present and devastated position of the socially assisted under-class has been identified as the most serious social problem of the time, as it is also the greatest threat to long-run peace and civility.
>
> Life in the great cities in general could be improved, and only will be improved, by public action—by better schools with better-paid teachers, by strong, well-financed welfare services, by counseling on drug addition, by employment training, by public investment in the housing that in no industrial country is provided for the poor by private enterprise, by adequately supported health care, recreational facilities, libraries and police. The question once again, much accommodating rhetoric to the contrary, is not what can be done but what will be paid.[16]

Unless substantial numbers of the people who need help exercise their right to vote, conditions will greatly worsen, as America slips ever deeper into decadence. Today America's true "preeminence" lies not in outer space but in failing to protect and care for her people. Little wonder that her cities are in desperate trouble.

It has been said that adoption of European planning and housing systems by the United States would be extremely difficult. The federal system of government and entrenched states rights are cited as tremendous obstacles, as are home rule and the predominant market-value approach to land and property decisions. We were getting close to the development of a national urban policy in 1973 when President Nixon eliminated urban renewal and a host of other programs. The pursuit of a national urban policy sank in the mist. For the sake of future generations, somehow it must be pursued again, somehow these obstacles must be overcome.

Components of my thesis have been borne out in some recent publications. In the January 1991 issue of *Planning* the then-president of American Planning Association, Stuart Meck, states that in recent speeches at regional and chapter conferences around the country, "I've been telling our members that planners 'are no longer weenies.' We are tougher, more pragmatic, and more interested in results than in high-toned talk."[17] If planners are "no longer weenies," the presumption must follow that heretofore they were weenies, less tough, less pragmatic, and more interested in high-toned talk than in results.

Urban planner William Fulton's informative and readable 1991 book *Guide to California Planning* gives the initial impression that planning in California might be farther along these days than it is on the East Coast. In response to Proposition 13's local government revenue restrictions (1978) and to California's ever-burgeoning population growth (6 million in-migrants in the 1980s), techniques including initiative and referendum ("ballot-box zoning") and municipal growth-control caps and ordinances are popular and plentiful. But so interested are citizens in low growth and other community matters (it is primarily special-interest citizen groups that put initiatives and referendums on ballots), that holding the planning process hostage over a dispute, or even litigation on the part of a disgruntled citizen group, is not uncommon. To the local planner, such active citizen participation may well seem at times to be a third major obstacle to good planning, along with resistant elected officials and developers.

Interestingly, for all the hundreds of municipal growth-control ordinances in California enacted in a recent period, the state's overall growth remained unreduced.[18] One of Fulton's reasons for stating that "the planning process simply doesn't work anymore"[19] is aggressive home rule that blocks needed regional planning. Another is the absence of a tax-sharing statute to prevent wild municipal competition for tax-paying development, as discussed here in Chapter 5. Fulton also finds basic planning goals gone awry.

Although American city planners are responsibly getting more and more into lobbying and testifying before subcommittees in Washington through the American Planning Association, at the local level planners are still being fired right and left for their positions on planning issues, according to 1990 and 1991 articles in *Planning*. This includes the planning director of Howard County, Maryland, Uri Avin, whose general plan for the county happened to win APA's Outstanding Planning Award for comprehensive planning in 1991. Asserting that he was not fired because of his planning skills, Avin's boss, the newly-elected county executive, was simply carrying out a campaign promise to fire Avin if elected![20]

City planning as constituted in America is like a tiny pilot fish swimming alongside a great shark. The economic system, the real estate business, home rule statutes, financial markets, political parties, government agencies, the labor movement, the corporate world, the interstate highway network—these, and others, are the great sharks of modern life.

American city planning is too insignificant to do more than flutter alongside one or another of these great sharks and try to look intelligent. But city planning's universe is huge and complex, composed of myriad interrelationships, structures that have evolved to different levels of maturity, and elements that are often unrelatable, moving at various rates of speed. This complex universe makes the need for a legally-empowered city planning profession even more acute. It makes the powerlessness of the profession all the more painful.

NOTES

1. N. R. Kleinfield with Michel Marriott, "On Stolen Wheels Newark Youths Defy Authority," *New York Times* (August 10, 1992), pp. A1, B5, and Michel Marriott, "For Idle Young in Newark, Pride in a Theft Done Right," *New York Times* (August 11, 1992), pp. A1, B4.

2. Mark S. Hoffman, ed., *The World Almanac*, p. 43; 1990 U.S. Population: 249.6 million.

3. Clifford Krauss, "House Passes Aid Plan for Inner Cities," *New York Times* (July 3, 1992), p. A10, and Editorial, *New York Times* (July 3, 1992), p. A24, and Editorial, *New York Times* (July 28, 1992), p. A26.

4. United States Conference of Mayors, news release (January 24, 1992).

5. Jerome Cramer, "The $40 Billion Controversy," *Time* (July 1, 1991), p. 11. NASA's chief at the time was Admiral Richard Truly.

6. Eric Pianin, "Space Station Funds Cleared by Senate Unit," *Washington Post* (July 11, 1991), p. A10.

7. PBS-TV, *Project Censored*, Bill Moyers. Dr. Helen Caldicott and a Soviet scientist (February 28, 1991).

8. Kevin Phillips, *The Politics of Rich and Poor* (New York: Random House, 1990), pp. 11, Appendix B.

9. U.S. Department of Education and UNESCO, by telephone, July 11, 1991.

10. "Bars and Stripes Forever," *Time* (January 14, 1991), p. 21.

11. PBS-TV, *Washington Week in Review*, Charles McDowell reporting (December 20, 1991).

12. Christine Gorman, "Listen Here, Mr. Big," *Time* (July 3, 1989), p. 40. Estimate attributed to a study by visiting Harvard Business School professor, sociologist Amitai Etzioni.)

13. Bruce W. Nelan, "Taking the Measure of American Racism," *Time* (November 12, 1990), pp. 16-17.

14. Archibald Cox, "Looking Ahead: Will the Dream Survive?" *Twenty Years of Citizen Action: Common Cause, 1970-1990*, 1990, pp. 29-30.

15. John Kenneth Galbraith, *The Culture of Contentment* (Boston: Houghton Mifflin Company, 1992), and PBS-TV, McNeil/Lehrer NewsHour, Robert McNeil Interview of Galbraith about this book (July 1, 1992).

16. Galbraith, *The Culture of Contentment*, pp. 180-81.

17. "From the Board," *Planning* (January 1991), p. 39.

18. William Fulton, *Guide to California Planning* (Point Arena, Calif.: Solano Press Books, 1991), p. 136.

19. Ibid., p. 263.

20. Mary Lou Gallagher, "Comprehensive Planning Award, Howard County 1990 General Plan," *Planning* (March 1991), p. 10.

Selected Bibliography

BOOKS

Adams, Henry. *Education of Henry Adams*. Boston: Houghton Mifflin Company, 1918.

_____. *Letters of Henry Adams, 1858-1891*. Ed. W. C. Ford. Boston: Houghton Mifflin Company, 1930.

Adams, Thomas. *Outline of Town and City Planning*. New York: Russell Sage Foundation, 1935.

Allen, Frederick Lewis. *The Big Change*. New York: Harper & Brothers, 1952.

Babington, Anthony. *The English Bastille*. New York: St. Martin's Press, 1971.

Bellamy, Edward. *Looking Backward*. New York: The New American Library, 1960. First published in 1888.

Bettman, Otto L. *The Good Old Days — They Were Terrible!* New York: Random House, 1974.

Bourne, L. S. *Urban Systems: Strategies for Regulation*. Oxford, England: Clarendon Press, 1975.

Commager, Henry Steele, ed. *Documents of American History*. Two-volume edition, Vol. I to 1898. New York: Appleton-Century-Crofts, 1968.

Davis, Rebecca Harding. *Atlantic Tales*. Boston: Ticknor & Fields, 1866.

Dreiser, Theodore. *A Book About Myself*. New York: Boni & Liveright, 1922.

Faulkner, Harold Underwood, and Tyler Kepner. *America, Its History and People*. New York: Harper & Brothers, 1938.

Fleming, Thomas. *The Man from Monticello*. New York: William Morrow & Co., Inc., 1969.

Fligstein, Neil. *Going North, Migration of Blacks and Whites from the South, 1900-1950*. New York: Academic Press, 1981.

Fulton, William. *Guide to California Planning*. Point Arena, Calif.: Solano Press Books, 1991.

Galbraith, John Kenneth. *The Culture of Contentment*. Boston: Houghton Mifflin Company, 1992.

Gallion, Arthur B., and Simon Eisner. *The Urban Pattern*. Fifth Edition. New York: Van Nostrand Reinhold Co, Inc., 1986.

Harrington, Michael. *The Other America*. Baltimore: Penguin Books, 1962.

Hecht, Marie B. *Odd Destiny, The Life of Alexander Hamilton*. New York: The MacMillan Publishing Co., Inc., 1982.

Hofstadter, Richard, William Miller, and Daniel Aaron. *The United States*. Englewood Cliffs, N.J.: Prentice-Hall, Inc., 1972.

Hommann, Mary. *Wooster Square Design*. New Haven, Conn.: New Haven Redevelopment Agency, 1965.

Howard, Ebenezer. *Garden Cities of Tomorrow*. London: Faber & Faber, Ltd. 1902.

Jacobs, Allan B. *Making City Planning Work*. Washington, DC/Chicago: American Planning Association, 1980.

James, Henry. *American Scene*. Ed. W. H. Auden. New York: Charles Scribner's Sons, 1946.

Kenyon, Thomas L., with Justine Blau, The National Alliance to End Homelessness. *What You Can Do to Help the Homeless*. New York: Simon & Schuster/Fireside, 1991.

Krueckeberg, Donald A., and Arthur L. Silvers. *Urban Planning Analysis: Methods and Models*. New York: John Wiley & Sons, Inc., 1974.

McDonald, Forest. *Alexander Hamilton*. New York: W. W. Norton & Co., 1979.

McLean, Mary, ed. *Local Planning Administration*, 3d ed. Chicago: International City Managers' Association, 1959.

McLuhan, T. C. *Touch the Earth. A Self-Portrait of Indian Existence*. New York: Promontory Press, 1971.

Mencken, H. L. *Prejudices, Sixth Series*. New York: Alfred A. Knopf, 1927.

Meyerson, Martin, and Edward C. Banfield. *Politics, Planning, and the Public Interest*. New York: The Free Press of Glencoe, 1955.

Miller, John C. *Alexander Hamilton: Portrait in Paradox*. New York: Harper & Brothers, 1959.

Mitchell, Broadus. *Alexander Hamilton, The National Adventure 1788-1804*. (One of several volumes.) New York: The MacMillan Company, 1962.

Mumford, Lewis. *The City in History*. New York: Harcourt Brace & World, Inc., 1961.

_____. *The Story of Utopias*. New York: Boni & Liveright, 1922.

Netzer, Dick. *Economics of the Property Tax*. Washington: The Brookings Institution, 1966.

The New York Times Company. *Report of the National Advisory Commission on Civil Disorders*. New York: Bantam Books, 1968.

Parton, James. *Life of Thomas Jefferson*. Boston: James R. Osgood & Co., 1874. Reprinted New York: DaCapo Press, 1971.

Peterson, Merrill D. *Thomas Jefferson and the New Nation*. New York: Oxford University Press, 1970.

Phillips, Kevin. *The Politics of Rich and Poor*. New York: Random House, 1990.

Poe, Edgar Allan. *Doings of Gotham*. Collected by Jacob E. Spannuth. Pottsville, Penn.: Jacob E. Spannuth, Publishers, 1929.

Quiett, Glenn Chesney. *They Built the West: An Epic of Rails and Cities.* New York: D. Appleton-Century Co., Inc., 1934.

Reps, John W. *The Making of Urban America.* Princeton, N.J.: Princeton University Press, 1965.

Riis, Jacob A. *How the Other Half Lives.* New York: Hill and Wang, Inc. Reprint 1957. Originally published in 1890.

_____. *Jacob Riis Revisited.* Ed. Francesco Cordasco. New York: Doubleday & Company, Inc., 1968.

Rudofsky, Bernard. *Streets for People.* Garden City, N.Y.: Doubleday & Co., Inc., 1964.

Savitch, H. V. *Post-Industrial Cities.* Princeton, N.J.: Princeton University Press, 1988.

Scargill, Ian. *Urban France.* New York: St. Martin's Press, 1983.

Scott, Mel. *American City Planning Since 1890.* Berkeley: University of California Press, 1969.

Smelser, Marshall. *The Democratic Republic 1801-1815.* New York: Harper & Row, 1968.

So, Frank S., Israel Stollman, Frank Beal, and David S. Arnold, eds. *Practice of Local Government Planning.* Washington: International City Managers' Association, in cooperation with American Planning Association, 1979.

Steffens, Lincoln. *The Shame of the Cities.* New York: Hill and Wang, Inc. Reprint 1957. Originally published by S. S. McClure Company, 1904.

Stone, Irving. *Clarence Darrow for the Defense.* New York: Bantam Books, 1965.

Tunnard, Christopher, and Henry Hope Reed. *American Skyline.* New York: Mentor Books, 1956.

Walker, Robert Averill. *The Planning Function in Urban Government.* Chicago: University of Chicago Press, 1950.

Webster's Guide to American History. Springfield, Mass.: G. & C. Merriam Company, 1971.

Weld, Theodore, and Angelina Grimké. *American Slavery As It Is*, 1839. Reprinted: New York: Arno Press and the *New York Times*, 1968.

Wharton, Edith. *A Backward Glance.* New York: D. Appleton-Century Co., Inc., 1934.

Whitman, Walt. Letter to "Pete." Quoted in William James. *Talks to Teachers on Psychology and to Students on Some of Life's Ideals.* New York: Henry Holt Company, 1899.

Whittick, Arnold. Editor-in-Chief. *Encyclopedia of Urban Planning.* New York: McGraw-Hill Book Company 1974.

ARTICLES AND OTHERS

Allen, Luther A. "British and French New Town Programs." *Comparative Social Research*, an annual publication. Ed. Richard F. Tomasson (Greenwich, Conn.: 1982), pp. 269-98.

Alsop, Stewart. "America the Ugly, Our Once-Lovely Land Has Become a Garish, Tasteless, Messy Junk Heap," *Saturday Evening Post* (June 23, 1962), pp. 9-10.

Belser, Karl. "The Making of Slurban America." *Cry California* (Fall 1970), pp. 1-21.

Cox, Archibald. "Looking Ahead: Will the Dream Survive?" *Twenty Years of Citizen Action: Common Cause 1970-1990.* Publication of Common Cause (1990), 29-30.

Davies, H.W.E. "Development Control in England." *Town Planning Review* (Liverpool, England: April 1988), pp. 127-36.

_____. "The Control of Development in the Netherlands." *Town Planning Review* (Liverpool, England: April 1988), pp. 207-25.

Edwards, D. "The Planning System and the Control of Development in Denmark." *Town Planning Review* (Liverpool, England: April 1988), pp. 137-58.

Ellis, Richard E. "The Political Economy of Thomas Jefferson." In *Thomas Jefferson, The Man . . . His World . . . His Influence.* Ed. Lally Weymouth. New York: G. P. Putnam's Sons, 1973, pp. 81-95.

Entwistle, Clive. "Total Habitat." *New York Times Book Review* (December 31, 1967), pp. 1, 18, 19.

Greenhouse, Steven. "Why Paris Works." *New York Times Magazine* (July 19, 1992), pp. 14-17, 24, 29, 49.

Harris, Britton. "Introduction: New Tools for Planning," *Journal of the American Institute of Planners* (May 1965), pp. 90-94.

Healey, Patsy. "The British Planning System and Managing the Urban Environment." *Town Planning Review* (October 1988), pp. 397-417.

Hommann, Mary. "Symbolic Bells in Dixwell." *Architectural Forum* (July–August 1966), pp. 54-59.

_____. "Letter to the Editor." *Pratt Planning Papers* (April 1963), p. 2.

_____. "Neighborhood Rehabilitation is Working in Six Projects in New Haven; Here's How." *Journal of Housing* (May 1962), pp. 186-88.

Johnston, Norman J. "A Preface to the Institute." *Journal of the American Institute of Planners* (August 1965), pp. 198-209.

Khakee, Abdul. "From Master Planning to Structural Planning." *Cities* (Oxford, England: November 1985), pp. 318-30.

Logue, Edward J. "Introduction." In *Survival Strategies, Paris and New York.* Ed. George G. Wynne (New Brunswick, N.J.: Transaction Books, 1979), pp. 7-19.

Lowry, Ira S. "A Short Course in Model Design." *Journal of the American Institute of Planners* (May 1965), pp. 158-65.

"National City Lines Guilty in Trust Case." *New York Times* (March 13, 1949), p. 79. (Prior *New York Times* reports on this case in 1949: February 16, p. 40; February 22, p. 36; February 23, p. 39; February 24, p. 37; and March 9, p. 44; in 1947: April 11, p. 38.)

O'Harrow, Dennis. *ASPO Newsletter* (Newsletter of American Society of Planning Officials). Editorial (August 1967), p. 2.

Peterson, Merrill D. "Thomas Jefferson: A Brief Life." In *Thomas Jefferson, The Man . . . His World . . . His Influence.* Ed. Lally Weymouth (New York: G. P. Putnam's Sons, 1973), pp. 13-37.

Pianin, Eric. "Space Station Funds Cleared by Senate Unit." *Washington Post* (July 11, 1991), p. A10.

Planning. Monthly periodical of the American Planning Association, Chicago, Ill.

Punter, John V. "Planning Control in France." *Town Planning Review* (April 1988), pp. 159-81.

Reinhold, Robert. "Drastic Steps are Voted to Reduce Southern California Air Pollution." *New York Times* (March 18, 1989), pp. 1, 8.

Rogers, Richard. "Capital Punishment." *Sunday Times Magazine* (London: March 1, 1992), pp. 16-24.

U.S. Courts—Abstracts of Cases:

    a. 68 S. Ct 1169 (1948).

       United States v. National City Lines, Inc., et al. United States Supreme Court. Decided April 28, 1948. (Issue of venue for the trial.)

    b. 186 F.2d 562 (1951).

       United States v. National City Lines, Inc., et al. United States Court of Appeals, Seventh Circuit. January 3, 1951. (The Court of Appeals upheld the 1949 convictions described in Chapter 9 herein. Because the 1949 trial was a jury trial, providing no judicial opinion, it was not abstracted in a federal digest.)

    c. 134 F. Supp. 350 (1955).

       United States of America v. National City Lines, Inc., et al. United States District Court, N.D. Illinois. September 19, 1955. (Injunction sought to forestall future violations.)

GOVERNMENT REPORTS

Abrams, Charles, ed. *Urban Land Problems and Policies.* United Nations, New York: Housing and Town and Country Planning, Bulletin 7, 1953.

Executive Office of the President, Office of Economic Opportunity. *Catalog of Federal Assistance Programs.* June 1, 1967.

Foreign and Commonwealth Office, U.K. *Planning, Urban Regeneration and Housing in Britain* (London: August/September 1990); and *Local Government in Britain* (London: April 1991).

Ministry of City Planning and Housing, French Republic and the United Nations Economic Commission for Europe, Committee on Housing Construction and Planning. *Human Habitation in France: Situation, Tendencies, and Policies.* New York: June 1982.

Public Law 101-625. 101st Congress, Nov. 28, 1990, the "Cranston–Gonzales National Affordable Housing Act," enacted by the Senate and House of Representatives of the United States of America in Congress assembled.

Rudberg, Eva. *Stockholm 1920-1985.* Stockholm, Swedish Museum of Architecture, Summer Exhibition, 1985.

Swedish Information Service. *Fact Sheets on Sweden.* Stockholm: October 1991 issue; and *Swedish News.* Stockholm: September 19, 1991, and October 4, 1991.

Swedish Ministry of Housing and Physical Planning. *Human Settlements in Sweden: Current Situation and Related Trends and Policies.* United Nations Economic Commission for Europe. 1982.

United Nations Economic Commission for Europe. *Methods and Techniques of Financing Housing in Europe.* Geneva, Switzerland: The Commission. 11 February, 1952.

United Nations, Department of Economic and Social Affairs. *World Housing Survey, 1974*. New York: A United Nations publication, 1976.

U.S. Department of Housing and Urban Development, Office of International Affairs. *Urban Growth Policies in Six European Countries*, a report presented to the Subcommittee on Housing of the Committee on Banking and Currency, House of Representatives. Washington, D.C.: November 1, 1972.

U.S. Department of Housing and Urban Development, Office of International Affairs. *HUD International, Information Series 20*. January 15, 1973. A newsletter.

REPORTS

Dolbeare, Cushing N. *Out of Reach*. Washington, D.C.: Low Income Housing Information Service, 1990.

———. *Summary of the Cranston–Gonzalez National Affordable Housing Act*. Washington, D.C.: Low-Income Housing Information Service and National Coalition for the Homeless. November 1990.

Stone, Michael E. *One-Third of a Nation*. Washington, D.C.: Economic Policy Institute, 1990.

Working Group on Housing. *The Right to Housing*. Washington, D.C.: Institute for Policy Studies, 1989.

Index

About the Author

MARY HOMMANN's forty-year career has included positions as Assistant Professor and Assistant Chair of the Department of City and Regional Planning at Pratt Institute, Development Planning Director for the City of Yonkers, Planning Director for the City of Long Beach, New York, and Director of the acclaimed Wooster Square urban renewal project in New Haven, Connecticut. She is a member of the American Institute of Certified Planners and the American Planning Association, and she is licensed to practice as a professional planner in New Jersey.